Endorsements

"Cyndi Targosz's energy is a marvel for women at any stage in their lives. Her passion for self-empowerment is bound to help women not only in love, but also in life. Cyndi's unflinching words in *Dating the Younger Man* help to dispel negative stereotypes of women. The reader emerges with the tools to be true to herself along with the courage to follow her heart."

—Laura Varon Brown, Editor,
Twist magazine, Detroit Free Press

"It doesn't matter if the man is older or the woman is older. The age difference makes *no* difference. True love is truly ageless . . . and so is Cyndi's take on it."

—John Rappaport, Producer/Head Writer,
M*A*S*H

"This is so much more than a book about boy toys. In her uplifting voice, Cyndi gives women of all ages the tools for finding their own way toward self-confidence, happiness, and ultimately love."

—Andrea Nobile-Westfall,
The Macomb Daily, Michigan

D1456517

Endorsements

"*Dating the Younger Man* lets women know that all of our options are open. It is a must-have guide for any woman who wants to try something new. Entertaining, insightful, and a lot of fun!"

—Marla Martenson,
author of *Excuse Me, Your Soul Mate is Waiting*,
www.marlamartenson.com, Beverly Hills Matchmaker

"In her newest book, *Dating the Younger Man*, lifestyle expert and image consultant Cyndi Targosz provides women of all ages with the tips and tools they need to find the younger men of their dreams. The sassy, no-frills dating guide encourages older women to flaunt their 'boy toys' and is chock full of successful May-December relationships that leave women feeling alive, empowered, and ready to take on the world!"

—Andrea Blum, Arts & Entertainment writer,
The News-Herald newspaper, Southgate, Michigan

"*Dating the Younger Man* is a delightful read with a dash of humor and a liberating message to all women about expanding their dating choices to include younger men. Old myths are dispelled. It's about ageless love for women, and it's about time."

—Pari Livermore, author of *How To Marry a Fabulous Man*,
San Francisco Matchmaker

Dating the Younger Man

A Complete Guide to Every
Woman's *Sweetest* Indulgence

Cyndi Targosz

Adamsmedia
Avon, Massachusetts

This book is dedicated to my mother, Helcia;
my father's "Little De-icer"!

• • •

Published by
Adams Media, an F+W Media Company
57 Littlefield Street, Avon, MA 02322. U.S.A.
www.adamsmedia.com

ISBN 10: 1-59869-668-8
ISBN 13: 978-1-59869-668-4

Printed in the United States of America.

J I H G F E D C B A

Library of Congress Cataloging-in-Publication Data
is available from the publisher.

This publication is designed to provide accurate and authoritative
information with regard to the subject matter covered. It is sold with
the understanding that the publisher is not engaged in rendering legal,
accounting, or other professional advice. If legal advice or other expert
assistance is required, the services of a competent professional person
should be sought.
—From a *Declaration of Principles* jointly adopted by a Committee of the
American Bar Association and a Committee of Publishers and Associations

Many of the designations used by manufacturers and sellers to distin-
guish their product are claimed as trademarks. Where those designations appear in this book and Adams Media was aware of a trademark
claim, the designations have been printed with initial capital letters.

This book is available at quantity discounts for bulk purchases.
For information, please call 1-800-289-0963.

Acknowledgments

Many wonderful people, including my family and friends, have supported me throughout my life and on this project. I wish to extend my sincere gratitude and thanks to all of them. Thank you to all the Boy Toys (BTs) and hot Boy Toy Babes (BTBs) who contributed their personal life experiences. All of you have enriched this program.

CONTENTS

67

Chapter 7

Friendly Flirting Made Easy

79

Chapter 8

Make the Connection

97

Chapter 9

The First Date (or the Last)

Advisory Note

The advice contained in this program is not intended to be a substitute for medical or psychological counseling. The program contains helpful guidelines for women dating younger men. Fictitious identities and names have been given to those interviewed and who responded to the cybersurvey in order to protect their privacy.

Introduction

My Dear Reader,

In your hands is the ultimate dating bible for women seeking relationships with younger men. I call it Cyndi's Secrets Boy Toy Program. With it, your odds of finding Mr. Right can increase tenfold. You now can choose from an even greater plethora of men of all ages. In the Boy Toy Program, I provide you with ideas on how to prepare to meet a Boy Toy, where to find potential partners, tips on securing your date with a Boy Toy, invaluable advice on overcoming the age difference, and ways to make your relationship with a younger man last. You might at first be a little hesitant about this concept. Don't fight it—enjoy it!

To begin, let me share a beautiful and intimate story:

It was early 1946. The big war had just ended and national pride was at an all-time high. The troops were finally coming home! *Boogie Woogie Bugle Boy* type music seemed to seep ceremoniously nonstop through the streets. Stanley J. Targosz, who was all of 25, could barely contain himself. He oozed excitement as he tripped up the porch steps to Helcia's house. He had traveled the world over while serving our country, managed to handle numerous brutal battles of the war, and was even one of the few heroes to survive the landing on Iwo Jima, with the image of the raised flag forever cemented in his mind. None of those engaging life experiences could even come close to his feelings for Helcia and the nervousness he felt over facing her that day. She was a beautiful, petite, 5' 2" strawberry blonde who held a spirit of fire, fun, and intelligence hidden beneath her fragile frame and dainty, quiet manner. He had been taken with her from the very moment when they had met four years earlier, just before he went into the service. Although they wrote to each other while he served our country, she kept him at bay. After all, a girl can't appear too available.

This was the day. Stanley was prepared to ask his beloved Helcia for her hand in marriage. Tall and handsome, he dressed properly in his best uniform. She melted at the sight of his broad and protective shoulders as he knelt down on one knee in front of the burning pot-belly stove in her father's living room. "Will you marry me?" Stanley asked Helcia with anxious anticipation. He did not expect a long pause. But there was nothing! No answer! No smooch—no nothing! Stanley went home a sad and very confused young man. Hey wait—that's not the way this story is supposed to end. Au contraire! To be continued—next paragraph.

It's true that Helcia did not say yes, but then again she also did not say no. Perhaps there was hope for young Stanley Targosz. The next day he went back with persistence to Helcia's house to profess his undying love. "Helcia," he said, "do you love me and will you marry me? Please let me know because I love you with my whole heart." Helcia began to cry.

After a silent moment, she lowered her head and sheepishly raised her eyes, hesitating as she said, "The reason I didn't tell you the other day is because I was scared. I was afraid because I am eleven months older than you." Without saying a word, he secured her tiny waist and scooped her up in his arms. They kissed with electricity that could have lit the sky like lightning. The magnetism lasted for fifty-five years of marriage, eight children, thirteen grandchildren, and two great-grandchildren. Till his dying day at age 80 he called her his "little de-icer" and, just weeks before his death on September 10, 2001, even recalled their first kiss. Stanley and Helcia became my parents.

Flash forward to today. It's hard to believe that anyone would think twice about marrying such a wonderful and handsome man. However, many women still feel guilty about caving in to carnal and emotional desires when it comes to choosing a man who makes the heart skip a beat—especially if he's younger. Wake up, girlfriend! I'm not talking about pretty-boy jerks who gaze in a mirror longer than I do, but rather tender, manly men who are secure in themselves. Handsome hunks who are ready to succumb to your every need and relish every level of your life experience. The revolutionary message that I deliver with passion is that ageless love can conquer all! It's just as easy to fall in love with a handsome and good man as an ugly and/or self-centered one. What's age got to do with it? Why not choose a man who fulfills you mentally, spiritually, and physically? Using my Boy Toy Program, you can emerge empowered and deliciously desirable. Of course, you must be willing to have fun along the way!

Remember back when women traded on their beauty and men traded on their wealth and power? A woman's only hope was to find a guy with money to take care of her. It didn't matter what kind of a person he was. Of course, not all rich guys are bad. However, in the old days, he could have been obnoxious, short, fat, and bald as long as he was rich. Many of these narcissistic guys did, and still do, think they are entitled to supermodels / beauty queens whom they can easily replace at the first sign of a wrinkle. Little do these buffoons know that their trophy women often cringe in the bedroom and even fake orgasms. In fact, it's more often than not that these trapped desperate housewives have to imagine a bag over *his* head.

Thankfully, the times are changing. As women grow more confident and financially independent, they are abandoning their mothers' "marry rich" mantra in favor of choosing a man who is rich both emotionally and physically. On top of that, he can still make a secure living or even be wealthy. According to studies of evolution and human behavior, the more independent a woman is, the more she values good looks in her man. Do not think for even a minute that I am promoting a relationship based strictly on looks or money— of course not! True love is what matters. However, why not have somebody who is good to you and rocks your boat at the same time? Modern women have seen too many of their sisters marry strictly for money, only to have miserable lives. My Boy Toy Program is not about eliminating older men from your wish list. It's about expanding your options. Men have done this for years. Why can't you?

Celebrities have been on the Boy Toy bandwagon for a long time. The media is saturated with images of Demi Moore and Ashton Kuchner, Halle Berry and Gabriel Aubry, and Madonna and Guy Ritchie, to name a few. With my celebrity secrets to Boy Toy bliss, you can be cherished for who you are, inside and out, at whatever age you are. There's nothing wrong with receiving pleasure from the man you choose. In fact, you should come to expect it. Of course, you should please him too. Until you feel that you deserve this preferential treatment, you will never achieve the ultimate love connection. Don't worry—I will be with you every step of the way. Follow my simple Boy Toy Program guidelines and you can become what I have coined a Hot Boy Toy Babe (BTB). You can leave behind any thoughts of living lonely, desperate days in despair. Rejoice in your newfound opportunity, and let the dating begin!

Love,
Cyndi

Chapter 1

The Investigation: Cybersurvey and Interviews

....
The Facts
....

I was approached one early October morning to put my Boy Toy Program into print. Certainly, my life experience, education as a certified lifestyle counselor, and being a relationship advisor were enough to make me jump with joy at the chance to share my feisty philosophy of ageless love. Heck, I've dated men of all ages, and relationship advice is my specialty. There is also a lot of current research being bandied about regarding the rise in women coupling with younger men. Studies shows that almost one-third of women between the ages of 40 and 69 are dating younger men. A recent AARP poll concluded that one-sixth of women in their 50s prefer men in their 40s. In addition to that, a national online survey recently stated that 51 percent of women do not care about age when looking for a mate. When you also take into account all the media frenzy around this topic, including network reality shows, news features, and celebrity hook-ups, you can only conclude that the opportunities to date a younger man have recently gotten better. That is great news—but not enough research for me!

I'm the kind of person who asks a lot of questions and gets to the bottom of everything. When I accepted this project, I felt driven to do my own research. It was imperative to connect with my readers on as personal a level as possible. I wanted to hear from real women just like you and their younger men—not just read some statistics. This was a job for Cyndi Sleuth. At first, I began interviewing men and women who are or have been in a relationship in which the man was younger. The discussions were fabulous, and the information incredibly valuable! However, even though my sampling was quite large and extremely beneficial, something in the depth of my soul wanted to dig deeper. See, I have always felt that a live interview could not avoid a slight margin of error. Experts say it can take months or even years before a client shares his or her whole truth. I wanted to be sure that my respondents were not just telling me what they thought I wanted to hear. My obsession was to dig even deeper and discover what was underneath their words—the "why." Then I had an epiphany!

Faster than you can download an MP3 tune, I sent out a dating "cybersurvey." First it went to family and friends, and then to the "Cyndi's Secrets" fan base from my Web site, *www.starglow.com*. I designed the survey for the men and/or women who are or have been in this type of relationship, whether married or dating.

There was a catch. What was the chance of the people receiving my survey being in this specific kind of relationship? Okay, here's where it gets zany! I encouraged the recipients of my opening e-mail to forward my survey to everyone in their address book, on the off chance that they might know someone who was, or had been, in a Boy Toy relationship. Wow—was I in for a shock! Within days of pressing "send," my mailbox was overloaded. The avalanche of responses just fueled the fire within me to deliver my powerful message and findings to you.

Taking research into this millennium is exciting. It was exhilarating to combine the information I gathered from my extensive live interviews with that from my cybersurveys. Admittedly, this was not a super-structured scientific study. I just wanted to hear from men and woman like you. The point is that with my cybersurvey, individuals felt free to speak from their hearts. And speak they did—some sent me pages and pages of thoughts. Others responded with short and to-the-point remarks. All of the replies via both the Internet and live interviews were extremely helpful, and I am grateful to all the respondents.

Following is a rough breakdown of the percentage of respondents based on gender and age. Remember that these people replied as individuals. It is possible that in some cases, their mate or mates did not respond.

Women	Men
Late 20s and 30s—20%	20s—33%
40s—29%	30s—30%
50s—28%	40s—28%
60s—21%	50s—8%
70s/80s—2%	60s/70s—1%

I asked my recipients to respond as individuals rather than as a couple to get honest feelings. My respondents could be totally anonymous if that was their desire. The dating cybersurvey provided a safe haven for deep thought and self-expression. I wanted the real scoop.

I did not set any rules as to how much younger the man had to be or how old the woman should be in order to participate in the survey and interviews. I promote an ageless agenda. Many women are even embarrassed to admit being in relationships in which they are only a year older. The majority of my respondents were in relationships in which the woman was between eight and twenty years older. Twenty-two percent of my respondents were in relationships in which the man was five years younger, or less. This often occurred when the woman was in her early 30s and the man in his 20s.

One surprise from this study is the huge amount of thought-provoking responses I got from women in their 30s. I knew that I would hear from women ages 40 and up. However, the wide age range of women who responded while proclaiming their right and joy in dating younger men was eye-opening. There was even a small percentage of women in their late 20s who responded because they were dating men in their early 20s. The fact that young women in their 20s put so much thought into my survey is a statement in itself. This shows that the dating double standard still exists, even for the younger women. The good news is that ageless love is on an upswing, and the relationships are working. In my Boy Toy Program, I provide guidelines for women of all ages regarding dating a younger man. Ladies—all of your voices are heard!

What the Research Means for You

After thinking about my personal experiences and reviewing the responses from my interviews and cybersurveys, I concluded that if you and other women seeking a man could be privy to the information collected, you could decide to embrace this liberating lifestyle choice. It expands your options for a mate. That's cool! I suspect the question in your mind is whether it can work for you. In the following sections, I'll explain why your answer may be yes. Don't worry if the information that I give makes you at first feel inadequate. I assure you that as you go through my Boy Toy Program, you will learn ways to help build your self-worth. For now, let's look at a few of the many reasons that a relationship with a younger man can be just the ticket.

Your Experience Is Exciting!

Let's face it—you probably have really lived life. Younger men cling to your every word and welcome your advice. The men in my study were unimpressed with the airhead qualities of some of their younger female counterparts. I heard the word "whiners" quite a bit when they described young women. Talk between a woman and her younger man proved to be a pleasure for the men in my study. These younger men love communicating, and actually enjoy hearing what their mate has to say. They raved about the woman's ability to contribute a mature point of view for mutual growth as individuals and as a couple.

You Are Hot!

Women are taking better care of themselves, and what can I say—guys are turned on by beauty at any age. You don't even have to be a perfect 10 to get their attention. They can tell if you are at your personal best, and that is the draw. The wrinkles mean nothing to them. In fact, many don't even have a clue as to what the age of a woman is when they meet her and frankly, they don't care!

Cyndi's Secrets™

A word of caution—always check to see if a potential Boy Toy is of legal age. Many underage boys look like handsome, mature men. Some of them may even lie to you about their age. You can always playfully ask to see his driver's license in addition to doing a Google search. Protect yourself and the underage boy from any possible criminal activity.

The Sex Is Great!

Now, don't blush. When it comes to sex, almost all the respondents, both men and women, said that lovemaking was off the charts! Sex was an almost unanimous big plus, or "+ + + +" as my respondents would type. In fact, the few times when it didn't go that well, it was because the woman was disappointed with her younger man. The majority of women preferred younger men because older men just could not keep up sexually. Younger men love the fact that an experienced woman knows her body and how to use it. Woo-hoo!

Confidence Is a Keyword!

The women in this study all exude confidence. I've worked as a celebrity image consultant in Hollywood for years, and know stars who struggle with the issue. I was so impressed with how strong, vibrant, and full of life the study participants were. To succeed in a relationship with a younger man, you must develop confidence. Again, don't worry—later in the program, I'll show you how to prepare. You can exude confidence and all the qualities necessary to attract and keep a good Boy Toy.

You Are Not Needy

These women are at a point in life where they are not needy. Many have financial security and established careers. Some have grown children. They revel in their independence and enjoy finally having the chance to meet their own needs. This is the time in life to find a man if you choose and, if you do so, for the right reasons.

He Is Active and Fun

Younger men tend to be more adventurous and not set in their ways. This is very appealing to women looking to have fun and lead an active life. You can discover life through each other's eyes.

Boy Toy Talk

"Ryan and I have been together a little over two years and going strong. He is nine years younger than I am. When I am being ridiculous about some circumstance from work or my life that's out of my control where I get frustrated, all he has to do is start giggling in his charming manner. I then realize that I am being ridiculous! It's great. No one has ever been able to 'teach' me that before. . . . I would normally just get mad at someone laughing, but he's really made it okay for me to laugh at myself and not take life so seriously! He laughs 'with' me, not at me!"

Rachel, 39

He Makes You Feel Young

There is a false myth that permeates our society: that dating a younger man makes you feel old. That is the furthest thing from the truth. The majority of my respondents felt younger because of their Boy Toy relationship. They felt totally worshiped and desired. I doubt if any woman would dismiss those feelings. Even in the long-term relationships, women remained feeling desired and young. In my study, the assumption that he won't want you when you get older did not hold water. Some of the younger men actually did not age as well as their female mates. What people fail to consider in these scenarios is that the age factor is relative. It's a simple truth—as you get older, so does he. Time has an equalizing effect.

Boy Toy Talk

"My husband was 23 when we met. I was 39. We married a year later. We have been married for fifteen years and are very happy. My husband is very good to me. He is very caring and loving. He will do anything to make me happy. He makes me feel beautiful and sexy, even though I am about thirty pounds overweight and sixteen years older. The age difference does not make any difference to my husband at all. It makes me feel younger to be with him. We are still happily married. We have a wonderful sex life. In fact, my husband wants me constantly. There are no minus points except my aging body, but my husband does not seem to care!"

Jolene, 55

A Boy Toy Babe Is Born!

There is an old stereotype of predatory women on the hunt for young meat. The word "cougar" seems to keep resurfacing. I personally do not like that image. It reeks of being the female counterpart to an old man who uses young women strictly for sex. The truth is that very few of the women in my study were the hunters. These younger men were in pursuit of them. Oh sure, some women have lured their Boy Toys in the way women have always done with men through the ages. However, a young man usually chases a woman because he thinks she's hot! Age was not an issue. This is quite a contrast to what transpires when a younger woman dates an older man. The older man is usually a symbol of long-term security. Of course, love is the foundation of many older man / younger woman relationships, so please don't think I'm being a snoot. Let's just stop the double standard. The biggest message is that love is ageless. Why not open your mind and heart to the option of a younger man in your life?

Let's crush the outdated "cougar" concept and adopt a more positive terminology. From this day forward, I christen you a hot Boy Toy Babe. Let the fun begin!

Boy Toy Talk

"I am 46 and Ben is 38. We've been together for two and a half years in a loving and committed relationship. Our age difference has not been that big of an issue. He says, 'Age is just a number.' He likes older women. Always has. I never thought I would be with someone eight years younger than me, but I was married to someone thirteen years older than I am, and believe me, younger is better! He teases me about being a 'cougar,' although I didn't pursue him. He pursued me! I rarely think about our age difference and what other people might think. We're comfortable together and very happy."

Christine, 46

Cyndi's Theory of Relativity

Here is a question to ponder. Let's say a 45-year-old Boy Toy is dating a 65-year-old hot BTB. She then leaves him for a younger 39-year-old Boy Toy. Then the 45-year-old man starts a relationship with a younger 25-year-old woman. Is he still a Boy Toy? Hmmm! Yes, dear reader, this is how I came up with Cyndi's Theory of Relativity. Simply stated— when it comes to Boy Toys in your life, it's all relative. By using my Boy Toy Program, the concept of a chronological number attached to a mature adult is nonexistent. Later in this program, I explain the various stages of men based on their age, and it is certainly extremely useful information. However, use it as a helpful guideline rather than a rule. The fact is that all of us on this planet are individuals who have lived past experiences that carve and shape our clay. The way you are molded and your very being are unique to you. Consider all the age-related factors when looking for your Boy Toy sculpture. However, take into account your individual needs and wants, coupled with his uniqueness. Only you know if the two of you can connect in mind, body, and spirit to complete the mix on the potter's wheel. It's the right ingredients rather than your ages that can create your personal masterpiece. Ageless love crosses all barriers. Time and space are not factors. It's all relative.

Chapter 2

Are You Too Old? The Truth

Finding Your Ageless Spirit

"Can I help you, ma'am?" What woman doesn't remember hearing that word for the first time? It usually occurs somewhere in the late 20s, and serves as a ritual into a new stage of life. How you respond to that realization depends on your attitude. Society says "60 is the new 40" and "40 is the new 30"! How liberating that sounds! Some things are changing for the good, and we should encourage this growth in our culture. This should be fabulous news, right? However, sometimes it's still like a slap in the face when a woman turns 30. She is chided into believing that it is downhill from there. Are you going to buy into that garbage?

Don't Be a Victim

To be a Boy Toy Babe with an ageless spirit, drop the poor victim role. It's not very appealing. Forget the 60/40, 40/30 age ratio stuff. I've heard the commercials and media messages sending out this "positive" message, and I fell for it, too. In fact, I was planning on raving about this new media message in this program. Truthfully, this is a positive message in the right direction, but something about it was nagging at me. It just felt like the age ratio comparisons were incomplete. Then, at about 3:00 A.M., as I was constructing this chapter, it hit me. That message implies that 40 is better than 60 and hey, 30 is even better yet. Being 30 years old is not better than being 40, or vice versa. Once again—don't buy into it! In part, this is just a marketing ploy used by companies to get you to buy their products. Each year of your life is a precious blessing filled with discovery. With my Boy Toy Program, you can start seeing yourself 20/20. Oh, I don't mean 20 years old. Start seeing yourself clearly as a perfect vision of the personal best you can be. Embrace an ageless spirit!

Developing this spirit can have its share of challenges. Following are a few real-life, depressing examples of the obstacles you may encounter. Perhaps deep down you feel like these women, or worse:

- **Latisha (33):** Her mom told her that she'd better hurry and find a guy or else she would end up an old maid.
- **Carmen (42):** Single and hoping to find a man, she is nearly convinced that her guy search is hopeless, her biological clock is nearly all run down, and she thinks she should just forget about it.
- **Clara (50):** When this attractive, successful attorney turned 50, she received a funeral arrangement from her peers. Though she laughed out loud, she was deeply hurt by this rude action.
- **Jane (64):** When she was younger, she felt confident about marrying Ralph. When he passed away five years ago, she never ever imagined she would be in the dating world again. This time around, she feels she has to settle for less.

- **Blanche (72):** After they'd been married for fifty years, Blanche's husband left her for a younger woman. In her mind, dating seemed out of the question.

Cyndi's Secrets™

Sarah was dating a 60-year-old man. One night he told her how happy he was with her zest for life. Dating her proved to him how important it was to never date a woman over 30. Sarah, who lived as an ageless spirit, never told him that she was 41. He assumed she was much younger. She could have used this ridiculous comment to bring her down. When a bomb hits you like that, rise above it. Needless to say, that relationship did not work out. Sarah is now seeing a fun and sensitive 38-year-old Boy Toy.

The Boy Toy Babe Plan

Okay—here is the plan. The next time you fall into a "poor me" pity slump, which we all do at times, take a deep breath and fight back. Start right this moment to see yourself as an ageless spirit. Just saying those words alone evokes a welcome sense of freedom. Shout it out: "I am an ageless spirit!" The burden of labeling yourself with a meaningless number is suddenly lifted and you are free to fly. If you can believe in your heart that an ageless spirit exists in your soul, you can overcome numerous limitations imposed by society. Your body can look hot! Your mind can continue to be stimulated, and your spirit can soar! With my Boy Toy Program, you can discover how to beat the odds at any age mentally, physically, and spiritually. One of the bonuses is that dating older men is no longer the limit. It's really quite exciting to know that you can increase the number of potential men in your life. Even more important is the discovery of true peace and happiness inside of *you*! I propose that all Boy Toy Babes revolt against any age-related negativity. When you hear the typical stereotyped comments about age, don't dismiss them. Speak out in your circle of friends and coworkers about how women are finally embracing their growth, sexuality, and life experience. If a commercial or news feature offends you, write the sponsor or news agency. If you are in the media, you are in a remarkable position to represent all sides of society. Boy Toy Babes of the world are pleading with you to include them in your stories in a positive light, alongside the youth culture. And remember, no one, including those of you in the media, are getting any younger. Chatter between ageless spirits can create awareness that leads to positive change. Revolt!

Make Your Own Rules

One night I was watching an extremely popular fashion makeover show when the host vehemently proclaimed, "Never wear a short skirt after 30." I scratched my head and gave my mini a little tug. I could hear my dad from heaven talking to me with the same parental tone he used when I was in junior high, high school, college, and well . . . till the day he died. He would say, "Cynnnnnthia, what is that you are wearing—a collar?" And yet here I was, sitting in the living room as a grown woman, getting scolded again, this time by the TV. Once the sound of my dad's voice dissipated from my mind, I thought about it for a brief moment—and I mean brief as in "millisecond"—"Am I too old to wear a miniskirt? Not! What's age got to do with it?" Dad would have agreed. Nowadays we still hear archaic advice like that about clothes, makeup, hair, and yes, the guys you date.

Shouldn't wearing a miniskirt be more about your personality and body type? Shouldn't who you date and/or have a lasting relationship with be about your personality, needs, and wants? I say make your own rules!

Maybe this sounds a little rebellious. I prefer to think of it as empowering. If you want to live your life as if it is already over, and that is your truth, go ahead. I choose a life of passion, love, fulfillment, growth, and tons of fun! Following my Boy Toy Program, you can too. This is not about miniskirts—I know that's not for everybody. This is about your truth. Find your truth in every decision that you make in life, including who you date.

With my Boy Toy Program, I give you some great guidelines so you can make the choices that are right for you. Forget rules that don't apply to you at this stage of life. You are a big girl now.

Ah—but there is one caveat: be responsible. For example, I think it is exhilarating that women are finally admitting that our sexuality is an essential part of our existence. That is part of why Boy Toys are so desirable. Almost every single one of the women in my research study raved about having great sex with her Boy Toy. However, I am not going to condone sleeping around with every Boy Toy you meet. That is your choice. If you decide to go that route, be grown-up enough to consider the consequences. There is the risk of getting or spreading sexually transmitted diseases; you might have an unwanted pregnancy; or dare I say it—you could break his heart, or even your own. When two consenting adults are making their own rules, it is critical to differentiate between lust and love. This can be particularly challenging when faced with his taut, strong shoulders and six-pack abs. If both parties know and understand the same truth, at least you are on a fair and honest playing field.

Cyndi's Secrets™

Having sex without a condom in a brand-new relationship does not make you fearless. It makes you stupid. Be a smart cookie and discuss safe sex before intimacy.

Making your own rules also means that you set standards as to how you expect your Boy Toy to behave. Although many older men don't want to believe this, women are capable of "just sex" too. Sure, it is true that our emotions play a major part in our femininity. I love that about being a woman. However, it's also true that society conditions us to be "good" girls, and at the same time to "let" cheating guys get away with their actions by claiming, "I can't help it—I'm a man." Pleazzzze! If you got caught with your panties down, would a man accept that excuse? The truth is this: whatever your age, or his, think highly enough about yourself to stop accepting double standards!

When it comes to relationships and dating, we all make mistakes. We are human. I've made some big-time doozies myself. The goal is to use those experiences to grow as an individual and as a couple. Make choices that are appropriate for you. Nobody knows your life as you do. Make your own rules for how you want to live life and how you expect to be treated. Once again, I repeat—be responsible! The golden rule "Do unto others as you would want others to do unto you" always applies. This brings me back to the original question of this chapter. Are you too old? What's *your* truth?

Kick into Confidence

While interviewing several Boy Toys for this program, I couldn't help but notice that one word repeatedly came up when they described why they love their Boy Toy Babe: confidence. I'm talking about real confidence, not the cocky bitchiness that's usually just a cover-up for hidden insecurities. A woman with a confident internal light that illuminates her world with life experience is a turn-on for men. Younger men in particular are drawn to a woman who has a sense of self-assurance. It radiates in her demeanor and the way she carries herself, and continues to shine through in her voice and in the words she says. You may be saying, "Oh no—that's not me!" I'm saying, "Yes, you can exude confidence at any age." Now that's a bright idea! Let me share why self-esteem is important, and what you can do to achieve it.

Boy Toy Talk

"I knew from the second I laid eyes on her that she was special. I wanted to hear everything she had to say. She wasn't needy or clingy like the younger girls I dated in the past. They just drained me. It was exhausting to constantly try to build up their self-esteem."

Jeff, 32

How Self-Esteem Applies to You

Good self-esteem forms the foundation of confidence. Having it means that you can take the hand that life dealt you and play it out to the fullest. Whether it's a royal flush or a pair of deuces, you are entitled to be happy, successful, and filled with love. Sure, we all have to face the ups and downs of life. That's just part of the game. By discovering how to cope and by taking solid steps to achieve personal fulfillment, you can be a winner regardless of the results. If you have a low opinion of yourself, it doesn't matter what you achieve, how much you acquire, or how good you look, because you will never think it's good enough. You see, it is the journey and how you perceive yourself in your own true light that trumps everything played out before you. Sometimes people who appear to have it all whether they are CEOs or movie stars are often the ones who have the lowest self-esteem. They usually end up never being satisfied. It isn't that having the drive or the enthusiasm for new challenges is a bad thing; striving to be your personal best is healthy. However, too many people, celebrities included, are walking through life in sadness due to low self-esteem. Sometimes you've got to wipe off that poker face and crack a smile! Start believing in your self-worth.

Boy Toy Talk

"I'm an entertainment industry consultant. Since I turned 40 almost ten years ago, I have almost exclusively dated much younger men (ranging from 21 to 45). Men my age can't seem to keep up with me sexually or physically, aren't in as good of shape as I am (which really isn't all that great), and often feel threatened by a successful older woman, preferring younger women who look up to them and don't challenge them. Younger men seem to find my sense of self and fun, and my independence, appealing, and generally aren't threatened by my intelligence or success."

Patrice, 49

Research shows that women are notorious for having low self-esteem problems. In fact, according to a Harvard University study, a vast majority of girls experience a shift in their self-image toward the negative in the middle school years, around or at age 12. At that point, the study says, educators see a drastic decrease in self-image and in academic achievement that they don't see in boys. Once puberty hits, the ability to be assertive, confident, and happy seems to lessen for many girls. Sometimes instead of getting better, it just keeps getting worse.

Check out your own life. How do you feel about yourself? This point is critical because self-esteem affects the core of your whole being. It affects how you manage your life at home, work, and school, and how you deal with people. It affects your level of success, and without a doubt your ability to have a quality relationship with a younger man. It is common for women with low self-esteem problems to put excess focus on "him." I have a friend who was going through a rough time in a bad marriage. I distinctly remember her telling me in a demure, quiet voice, "I guess I should be happy. After all, he did *choose* me." This subtle nuance packs a punch. It screams a sense of settling for less. The operative word is "choose." To succeed in a mature and healthy relationship with a younger man, be sure that it starts with "lady's choice." If the two of you click, how wonderful it is to know that you chose each other. This is a healthy way to safeguard your self-worth and to respect each other.

Cyndi's Secrets to Good Self-Esteem

To develop good self-esteem, follow these tips:

- **Get real!** Take a look at yourself from a realistic point of view. Perhaps at 50 you didn't achieve the net worth you thought you would. Maybe your marriage failed and the dream isn't going the way you planned. It is what it is. You still deserve to be happy. Okay—new plan! Move on!
- **Follow your gut.** People with high self-esteem have discovered the value of following their intuition. It's usually right.
- **Admit your boo-boos.** Everybody screws up every now and again. It takes a strong woman to say, "I made a mistake."
- **Bend and stretch.** Being flexible goes beyond a yoga class. It's having the ability to change when it is necessary. Sure, you may have to work through a few kinks. Life is way too short to let yourself get out of joint.
- **Be independent.** The more independent you are, the better your self-esteem. Of course we all are vulnerable at times, but with independence, the difficult times aren't as hard to take.
- **Get along.** The luckiest people on this earth are those who need other people. Cherish your true friends for they can remind you how special you are.
- **Nurture your talents.** One of the greatest confidence boosters is to develop your God-given talents to the best of your ability. This is tremendously fulfilling and fun—and the guys find it seductive.

Become a Fearless Female

Kicking into confidence is not for the scaredy-cats of the world. It takes a fun, fearless female to roar with the courage of a lioness. This doesn't mean you should jump off of a bridge, pick up a hitchhiker, or put yourself in harm's way. One must always exercise caution. However, being afraid to put yourself out there holds you back from experiencing much of what life has to offer. Sometimes you just have to let yourself out of the cage and have fun prowling. I know there are a zillion things to be afraid of when dating, and the pressure is even higher when you think of that birth year on his driver's license. What will people think? Am I too old? Questions like this, coupled with the possibility of facing rejection, can linger in your mind. Okay, then—close this book. Stay home and forget about it all. Silly girl—I know that seems much safer, but it doesn't sound like very much fun.

Living Happily Ever After

The reality is that some people may be shocked by the fact that you are much older than your Boy Toy. Some may think you are fat, old, and in need of a nose job. These things could even be true. Your Boy Toy may even turn out to be a jerk and leave you snarling in the dust. Guess what—that still sounds like more fun than staying home! Of course, it is always your choice. Did I forget to mention that you could meet a great guy who rocks your boat and you live *happily ever after*?

I know, modern women are not supposed to believe in the fairy-tale ending. However, most of us dream about it. I am saying you *can* have that dream. When you face the world as a fun, fearless female with confidence, you are prepared to take on and deal with any challenges that come your way. No one, and I mean no one, has the right to take your joy away from you unless you let them. Don't let them. With this kind of attitude you can be happy while you are married, single, or in any relationship. I'm not talking phony

Pollyanna positivism. Rather, it's calmness that comes from knowing you are not afraid to really live! With this state of mind, you *can* live happily ever after. Sleep well, sweet princess, whether alone or with Prince Charming.

Gusto Inside and Out

The steps to being fearless require that you go forward with great gusto. Discover how to kick into confidence by working on your inside and your outside.

THE INSIDE STORY

Working on your inside is a great way to start fighting fear. First, make a list of your talents—the things you do really well, or nice qualities that you possess. And don't say there is nothing, because everybody is good at something. Maybe you're a great swimmer, a loyal friend, or one hell of a kitchen cabinet organizer. It can be anything; just concentrate on something positive about yourself. This is no time to feel sorry for yourself, so if you really can't think of any talents or nice qualities about yourself, ask a friend or try a coworker. You know—the sweet but dorky guy you have no interest in but who fawns over you at the water cooler. He'll provide you with a long list. This is just a start to help you overcome fear. Keep developing your talents and try new skills. Research shows that becoming skilled in something you love to do can help to carry over in all areas of life. Hey—dating younger men is sure to help you build your confidence!

OUTSIDE THE BOX

People always say you should think outside the box. This often applies to your job, but also don't be afraid to think outside the box when it comes to appearance. Say what you want, but appearances do count to some degree. Why not present yourself in a way that represents you at your best? I'll show you in the upcoming chapters how you can improve your looks, stay true to you, and rev up your confidence at the same time.

Taking It to the Streets

So far I've shared with you the importance of achieving good self-esteem and explained how you can achieve it. We talked about the fun of being fearless and having the tools to kick into confidence as an ageless spirit. Now it is time to take it to the streets and put these new attitudes into practice. I realize putting yourself out in the world with this new attitude may seem like risky business. You can do it. Search for opportunities that bring purpose and joy in your life. Whether it's dating younger men or taking up scuba diving, just get out there. Always honor yourself. As you make this critical step I remind you of what Shakespeare wrote in *Hamlet*: "This above all: to thine own self be true." Stay true to you.

Chapter 3

Leave Loneliness Behind

This One's for Lonely Hearts

If you are lonely, you are not alone. Everybody has those empty feelings at one time or another. That is just a part of life. It's common to feel isolated when you are alone at home, work, or wherever you may be. It's also just as common to feel alone in a crowded room. Feeling alone spurs a false sense of being inadequate. Living in a society that promotes coupling can add to this insecurity. Go ahead and blame the precedent set by Noah's ark if you like, but the key is to make sure that these feelings do not overwhelm you or interfere with living a healthy, balanced life. Not only can this mess up all areas of your daily life, but it can destroy any chance of attracting a younger man.

Okay—let's hit this topic head-on. If your heart is heavy, let me help you find out what's really causing the despair. You can address your feelings and I'll help you discover some ways to manage them. First, think about what is causing the loneliness. This is very personal. I've listed a few possibilities for you to ponder:

- Perhaps you are currently single and are experiencing thoughts of incompleteness.
- Are there group activities or events that you don't feel a part of? For example, you may have been invited to a wedding but don't have a significant other to bring to the event.
- Your surroundings just don't seem connected to you. It's as if you are out of place.
- You don't have a trusty friend to share your emotions and life experiences.

Once you have pinpointed the source of your loneliness, dig a little deeper. What emotions does this loneliness make you feel: anger, isolation, insecurity, self-doubt, self-loathing? Having feelings like these can really do a number on your disposition. You could even plummet to low self-esteem or severe depression. Some people who feel like this eventually refrain from social activities. They are convinced that nobody wants to be around them anyway. Others do not know how to assert themselves and never say no. This indirectly enhances the lonely feeling because it causes them to feel exploited.

Loneliness manifests itself in numerous ways. Let's explore what you can do to combat loneliness.

Cyndi's Secrets™

Here is a word of caution. There are men who find girls in the lonely-hearts club extremely attractive. These men generally are control freaks and see heartache as a chance to manipulate. Be careful if you are in a lonely and vulnerable state of mind. Make sure that his intentions are good.

....
What You Can Do about Loneliness
....

All right, I promised you a program that gets results. To get the best Boy Toy of your dreams and feel better about yourself, you need to manage your loneliness. With my program, you can find the path that abolishes any self-pity patterns. I offer guidelines to get you on the right track. There is also advice about seeking professional help if need be. So quit wallowing in your sorrow and put this plan into action!

A Survival Strategy

If you were stranded on a deserted island, you would need a survival strategy. Take a good look at yourself. Incorporate information from this chapter into your daily life. Be confident that with a little practice, you can be a winning survivor.

Here are some great tips to help you overcome any feelings of isolation:

- **Remember—everybody gets lonely.** Everybody feels lonely at one time or another. This is only natural. It's actually your mind's way of sending you a message. It could be saying, "Hey, you have needs that are not being met!" It could be telling you to make some changes. Perhaps you need to make some new friends, or develop constructive ways to be alone without being lonely. It's up to you to listen to what your mind is saying. Only you know what your needs are. Discover what action can take you out of the doldrums and into a Boy Toy–ready state of self-acceptance.
- **Speak up!** Be the first to say hello. Most people, and especially Boy Toys, love to be acknowledged. Psychologically this behavior can help you feel like you

are a part of the race. It may be the rat race, but at least you belong, and that's not quite as lonely.

- **Smile. Smile, smile, smile!** Smile at people on the elevator, in the line at the bank, or running in to your next appointment. The energy is contagious. The feeling of loneliness can dissipate even if you never actually get to know these people by name. The late comedic actor W. C. Fields once said, "Start every day off with a smile and get it over with." However, studies show that a smiling person is perceived to be more attractive, sincere, competent, and sociable than a nonsmiling person. Smiling even releases endorphins that can make you feel better. So get going with that grin. Smile extra wide when your eyes meet up with a potential hot Boy Toy mate. "We shall never know all the good that a simple smile can do," said Mother Teresa. Who can argue with that?

- **Beseen.** Get involved with people and activities that are of interest to you. Join an organization, participate in a sport, or volunteer to do something that you enjoy. What a great way to meet guys, combat loneliness, and just feel better about yourself. A word of caution—life is about balance. I sometimes think it is just as harmful to overload your schedule with tons of activities. You may think that this keeps you busy and that you are being seen in public. However, people who have an overcrowded schedule can actually be very alone. If you have overextended your schedule, ask yourself, "Are my needs getting met?" If being active is really to cover up a fear of being alone, it's time to face up to your loneliness.

- **Build friendships.** Remember that intimacy takes time to build. Be a good and kind friend to others. Practice patience. Some women think that if they find romance, the loneliness will disappear. They are convinced this will take them up a step on the self-esteem and social ladder. If you are depending on romance to combat loneliness, you might as well walk under that ladder. You are setting yourself up for bad luck in love. It is imperative to be a friend first.
- **Don'tfake it!** Don't fake an interest in others and in various activities. Gravitate to people who genuinely have similar interests. Some people like to socialize in groups, while others prefer one-to-one communication. Once again—be true to you!
- **Ditch deprivation.** If you can't find somebody to do an activity with, go ahead and do it anyway (for example, try going solo to a movie, art show, or concert). This can boost your confidence and combat the lonely blues. Traveling as much as I do can sometimes be lonely. I've discovered a great sense of empowerment by doing a number of activities on my own, such as having dinner in a fancy restaurant. I walk in the room with kindness but won't accept a bad table, never apologize for being alone, and relish the attention that a confident woman can command. Suddenly I am no longer lonely. This is a great way to meet a lot of fascinating people. It's really quite fun!

Boy Toy Talk

"As a studied art historian, I love to spend hours at my favorite museums in the city. My friends don't share the same love, and it was frustrating always trying to find someone to enjoy the experience. I started going alone and discovered I preferred my newfound tranquility. One Wednesday morning as I stared at a chaotic Kandinski painting, Bill offered his impression of the piece. I found his forward manner quite charming. Although he preferred Picasso, we both had plenty to discuss. That was five years ago. We still debate Dali, but revere Renoir. He is ten years younger than me."

Kristine, 45

Counseling Can Help

Some people suffer from extreme bouts of loneliness that can interfere with daily life. This feeling of isolation may or may not be related to clinical depression. Only a trained mental health professional can make that conclusion and provide the appropriate diagnosis. There is a wide range of so-called mood disorders that run the gamut of mild to extremely severe. It could be that an individual suffering loneliness just needs to talk it out with a therapist. In any case, if you are experiencing severe loneliness or feelings of unremitting sadness, be sure to seek professional help.

GROUP COUNSELING

Group counseling can be very helpful if you are fighting feelings of loneliness. It can be comforting to meet others who have similar emotions. Members in the group are encouraged by the therapist to be supportive of each other. This should be a safe environment in which to explore the hidden issues causing depression and loneliness.

INDIVIDUAL COUNSELING

One-to-one counseling can also be therapeutic. Talking to the therapist can help you discover what is underneath the emptiness you may be feeling. She can help you understand yourself better and explain how to adapt a new and healthier attitude. She can show you how to chill when faced with meeting new people in social situations.

Some therapists like to use cognitive-behavioral techniques when conquering loneliness. For example, if you panic every time a younger love interest passes by, your therapist may suggest a plan to help overcome anxiety. A trained therapist can help you create positive thoughts to replace the negative thought patterns. Do not be afraid to seek help if you need it. Sometimes it takes therapy *on* the couch to get you *off* of it!

Cyndi's Secrets™

Forget lonely Saturday nights. Invite a few friends over for a "Book and Cook Club" party. These fun evenings are popping up everywhere. Everybody helps to prepare a healthy meal and discusses a favorite book. Try talking about *Dating the Younger Man!*

Make a Date with Yourself

In every woman's life there comes a morning when she wakes up alone and looks at the clock. She then realizes it's Sunday morning. Not just any Sunday morning, but the Sunday morning that comes after a dateless Saturday night. Alone and bewildered, she wonders how this could happen to her again. How humiliating! I say to you—wake up and get over it! When you discover the joy of making a date with yourself, you can overcome loneliness. One of the biggest of Cyndi's Secrets is the ability to love yourself enough to take "you" out on a date. With this secret, I can guarantee that you will never be dateless again. The fringe benefit is that this attitude can carry over into your entire disposition. Suddenly you can become very appealing. Nothing turns men off more than a desperate woman on the hunt. I don't care if you look super-hot, they will still run. Oh, you might get a one-night stand, but to be the object of a man's deepest desire you've got to love yourself. Go ahead and make a date with yourself. It's okay to choose to stay home on Saturday nights. I actually enjoy choosing to have an occasional Saturday night to myself (even if someone has asked me out).

Having a plan ahead of time can help you to keep a positive attitude. It's too easy to start feeling sorry for yourself. Make sure you decide to do something that you really enjoy. This way you can look forward to your date with "you." Here are a few ideas that can make a Saturday night extra special:

- **Takea bubble bath.** Relax in a long, luxurious bath with your favorite soaks. Light candles and listen to music that lifts your spirit. Afterward, be sure to saturate your skin with the finest oils and creams. Finish with your favorite scent.
- **Preparea meal that would win the heart of any date.** In this case, it is the most important heart of all—your own. Bring out the finest china and silverware, and set a fabulous table. Light the candles. Take your time. Choose foods that are healthy, delicious, and filling. Nurture yourself. Just be careful that the spread for "you" doesn't spread you.

- **Rent a DVD.** Curl up on the sofa with a cup of herbal tea and a chick flick. Keep Kleenex nearby. Or go ahead and view those old episodes of the Three Stooges you love to watch. Indulge in your guilty pleasures.
- **Go out!** Nobody says you can't take yourself out. Do whatever your little heart desires: in-line skating, the movies, shopping, or whatever.
- **Organize your photo album.** Many people store photos in boxes with the intention of sorting the pictures some other time. Some have their photos in computer files that are a digital mess. Have fun accomplishing a task that could stir up some warm fuzzy feelings and is a productive thing to do. However, I'd skip the shoebox with the ex-husband's photos. A fire may be a better idea for those. Just kidding—maybe!
- **Read a delicious steamy novel.** Slide back on your recliner and have a sweet escape.

Whatever you decide to do on Saturday night, or any night for that matter, you now have what it takes to manage loneliness. Spending more quality time alone has tons of wonderful benefits. You can discover things about yourself that you didn't know existed. Perhaps you have a knack for painting or playing the piano. Just be sure you enjoy your time. This can boost your confidence tenfold. When you like yourself a lot, and I mean a *lot*, the whole world will like you more too—including Boy Toys!

Chapter 4

Unleash the Goddess Within

....
Live Life with Passion
....

Preparing to be a Boy Toy magnet takes confidence, an ageless spirit, and certainly the ability to overcome loneliness.
However, to catch the Boy Toy of your dreams you also need
to unleash the goddess within. So many women hide their
inner light without realizing it. Why is it that some women
can walk into a room and everybody clamors for their attention? You know the type. She enters the restaurant. Heads
turn. Her aura is brilliant and everyone wants to be near
her. She is not necessarily an extraordinary beauty, but she is
extraordinary. Her beauty goes beyond her outside appearance. She is a goddess. You can be one too! Every woman
has the ability to unleash the goddess within. It only requires
that you live your life with passion. I'm talking about having
enthusiasm about everything you do, from the moment you
awake till the second you drift off to sleep.

What is passionate for one woman may not be for
another—that is the beauty of "you." Putting passion in your
life is like having your own personal perfume. It serves as
an aphrodisiac. Once you let it out of the bottle, it is intoxicating. Quit hiding all the potential built up inside of you.

You can dab a little passion in your life. It'll make you feel sensational and it'll knock that Boy Toy out!

Cyndi's Secrets™

Many of the Boy Toys in my survey were attracted to women who were in touch with their sensuality. They expressed dissatisfaction with younger women who hadn't lived long enough to understand the indulgence in the simple pleasures of life.

Developing your inner goddess goes beyond having good self-esteem. Goddesses possess an extra-special air, and I'm not talking perfume. It's striving to reach your highest potential while practicing kindness and good deeds. It requires that you use your sensuality as one of your greatest assets. Explore all of your senses: taste, touch, smell, sight, and sound. Notice that I said "sensuality," not "sexuality." Sensuality has to do with indulging in the pleasure of your senses while sex is—well, sex. Sensuality is about *you* living a life of passion! Okay, it's true—Boy Toys just happen to find a woman who's in touch with her sensuality and living life to the fullest "sexy"! This is where you can have the edge over your younger counterparts. Your life experience can help you tap into your senses with ease. Sophia Loren comes to mind. When she was 72, *People* magazine named her number six on its "most beautiful" list. That same year she also appeared in the famous Pirelli Calendar, which is famous for attracting the world's most glamorous actresses and models. According to much of the media, she was the most beautiful in the calendar. That's a goddess! Now get ready to unleash the goddess within you.

My program provides you with useful information to reach your highest BTB potential. I want to push you to your limits. It's time to take a realistic look at yourself and develop a plan of action for self-improvement. With this Boy Toy Program, you can whip up your own personal make-over plan. Why not feel good about yourself and capture the heart of a gorgeous hunk at the same time? Enough with the words—let's get to work. Use your passion as the link between your dreams and your achievements. It all starts with balance.

Beginning with Balance

Remember the excitement of getting your first bicycle, complete with bell and training wheels? Probably like most children, you couldn't wait to learn to ride it. The training wheels made you feel safe and secure for a while. Before long, you most likely wanted them taken off so you could ride "like a big girl." Finally, the day came when your dad removed the trainers. He told you not to worry, because he would hold on to the back. Oh—the astonishment and delight when you turned and discovered he wasn't there, and you were riding on your own. You were free and confident and never looked back. That kind of exuberance and grace can only occur with "balance."

If balancing on a bike could do so much for your self-esteem as a child, just imagine what balance in your life can do for unleashing the goddess within. Having a balanced lifestyle can increase your man magnetism and, to an even greater degree, your overall well-being. To help you do this I have developed the M.B.S. System (Mind, Body, Spirit). I use this system in everything I do. It is a constant thread throughout my life and inherent throughout the Boy Toy Program.

Let's take a look at the three parts of the M.B.S. System:

- **Mind:** A mind sharp and constantly stimulated is sexy.
- **Body:** Love your body enough to take care of it inside and out. With a younger guy you may be more body-conscious. Make it the best it can be.
- **Spirit:** This is the part that deals with your feelings and attitudes.

Using the M.B.S. System can help you think, look, and feel your best as you enjoy the journey toward your goals. If any part of this triad is off kilter, the whole system falters and you wobble. There are concrete and specific things that you can do to strengthen every part of this threesome to keep you strong, secure, and ultimately balanced. In this chapter, I explain how you can develop these three integral components. Use this information to unleash the goddess within you—to create your personal makeover plan. It's time to get back on that bike and ride through life with balance. The cool part is now that you are a big girl you can do all the wheelies you want. Hey—you may even need a bicycle built for two. Now that's the real balancing act!

Mind Matters

"Nice ass!" "Great tits!" "Those legs go on for miles!" "Wow! Did you get a look at her brain?" Okay—the last comment may not be the most-heard wolf howl on the street. However, don't kid yourself into thinking that playing dumb is the way to go to catch a Boy Toy. The secret that every goddess knows is that mind matters do matter. To get the edge in the goddess department, developing your mind is pretty darn smart, and it's really hot, too! Younger guys have been raised by a generation of women who taught them to respect a smart woman. They are attracted to a sexy siren who can carry on a meaningful conversation. Regardless of whether you date an older or younger man, it behooves you to do everything in your power to develop your knowledge base and improve your memory and cognitive ability.

Boy Toy Talk

"Age is an issue of mind over matter. If you don't mind, it doesn't matter."

Mark Twain

Mental Fitness

To stay young in the mind, mental fitness needs to be a part of your daily life. Let me explain. Your brain is an organ that continues to think and grow even as you age. It has the ability to develop new neurons into the later years. The key is that you have to keep stimulating it. Mental fitness improves your mind in the way that exercise improves your body. This can further enhance the way your brain functions. The lack of mental fitness or stimulation can cause memory loss or cognitive decline. In a nutshell—use it or lose it. This is great news for a Boy Toy Babe determined to stay young at heart. Exercise your mind with the following mental fitness routine:

- **Never Stop Learning:** Before I graduated from college, I learned a very important life lesson. The classes and teachers helped me to know how much I don't know. Never lose your desire to keep learning. Delight in the discovery of all that is new to you. Read everything you can get your hands on. Take classes. Ask lots of questions.

- **Improve Short-Term Memory:** Stimulate your short-term memory by trying to recall recent occurrences. You could make a mental note of all the items you just had for lunch with your girlfriends. Remember the herbs, seasonings, flavor, and aroma.
- **Improve Long-Term Memory:** Challenge your long-term memory by retracing experiences. Recall the items and details of the lunch you had with your girlfriends a week ago.
- **Switch Hands:** Switch hands when doing your daily activities. For example, if you open the door with your right hand, try it with your left. Don't worry if this feels awkward. The new activity stimulates the neural connections in your brain and even creates new ones.
- **Play Games:** Exercise your mental logic by playing games. Puzzles, cards, and chess are but a few mind-stimulating activities. Try to play different types of games to challenge different parts of your logic.
- **Report:** Use your verbal abilities to report what you remember. If you watch TV or listen to the news in the morning, you can share the information with someone in the evening. This provides mental stimulation for both parties.
- **Build Your Vocabulary:** Try to increase your vocabulary. If you see or hear a word that you don't understand, find out what it means. The dictionary is your friend.

There are many ways to stimulate your mind. Try going to the grocery store without a list. Memorize faces and names. Recall phone numbers. Take a different route home. Travel and discover. Use your brain!

Food for Thought

Good nutrition can affect your inner goddess potential. In fact, some foods do much to nourish the brain. Proteins stimulate the cells to keep you communicating with clarity. Fatty acids allow you to think and feel. Carbohydrates provide the glucose that motivates you. Fruits and veggies supply the antioxidants for brain cell repair. For more information about the brain, visit the Franklin Institute, which is based in Philadelphia, at *www.fi.edu/brain/diet.htm.*

Cyndi's Secrets™

A hot BTB should never underestimate the value of good nutrition. This is not to say you have to starve yourself to get a bony ass. No way! I love food! I say embrace your unique feminine curves. Pick up a copy of my book *The Only Diet Book You'll Ever Need.* It's the secret to eating well, losing weight, and loving life. It's your life—make it a delicious one!

Body Beautiful

Your body is the second part of the M.B.S. System. The female form is a masterpiece of nature. Women come in so many different shapes and sizes, and each creation is unique unto herself. Yet it seems that women never are happy with their bodies. Eighty percent of women see themselves as fat. This is sad. To unleash the goddess within, you need to love yourself—inside and out. Did you notice that I said both "inside and out"? There is an ongoing battle in society. In one corner, having a good body image, being happy with the body you have, is the answer to everything. Just love yourself, the feel-good types say. The other camp says you should do everything you can to be skinny, hot, and young looking. The fight persists between the internal strength of a good body image versus the external power of a bod that rocks.

This dichotomy used to bewilder me. My specialized training as a body image expert and my personal philosophy make me passionate about helping you and others cultivate a healthy body image. Beauty comes in lots of different shapes and sizes. On the flip side, having worked as a model I care a lot about my looks. In fact, I know tons of beauty and fashion secrets that I try to use to my full advantage. The point is that regardless of how healthy someone's body image may be, looks do matter. These days I know not to judge a book by its cover. However, I also know that the cover can help to sell the book. By achieving your personal best inside and out, you can improve your body image tenfold. Your odds of attracting a younger man go up too. Let's look at it this way. If you don't attract a Boy Toy with your outside, he may never get the chance to open your book, or you his. Let me share my secrets to the true potential of your Boy Toy Babe body. Regardless of what nature gave you, you can have great looks and feel wonderful about yourself, too. Let your chapters unfold.

Feel Sexy Naked

The way you perceive yourself determines your body image. Thus, if you perceive yourself in a positive light, you have a healthy body image. Seeing yourself as a fat and wilted old prune that is all washed up would be a bad body image. Okay, so it's not always that clear-cut. For most people, a healthy body image is a daily struggle. Some of my clients who are hot actress/model types have the biggest body image problems. They have so much pressure to be "perfect." It's impossible for them to live up to the digitally touched-up images of themselves. They constantly overhear comments like "She doesn't look as good in person." I tell you this because nobody is perfect, supermodels included. It may sound like a cliché, but still, true beauty does begin from within. None of the beauty secrets that I or anyone else can give you is worth a dime if you don't work on the goddess within first. Consider the natural progression of getting older. Aging can be hell if you don't like yourself. Let me give you *inside beauty* Cyndi's Secrets to feeling sexy and sensational in your "buck-naked" Boy Toy Babe body. Work at this every single day.

EMBRACEABLE YOU

The first step is to embrace your ever-changing body. Love it during puberty, PMS, menstruation, pregnancy, and menopause. Love it during every feminine form it takes. Okay—fat days may be extra hard to take. So, suck it in! Most women waste too much time fretting over natural female transformations. One of my celebrity clients is a high-profile actress who asked to remain anonymous. She has legions of fans, and when you see her on TV or in the media, you would never believe that she has suffered from a body image problem, which almost prevented her from marrying a wonderful Boy Toy. She wanted you to hear her story.

"At 35 my resume was looking good and I felt relatively happy. Even if some of the work tapered off, I figured it was just a dry spell. It happens all the time in this business. My agent called me in one morning for a meeting. Apparently I lost a role that I was perfect for to another actress—because I was too 'camera heavy,' he said. That is a death sentence in my work. All I could hear in my mind was, 'I'm fat!' No nice terms can make that sound better! I already felt lousy about my physical appearance, and this just compounded my problem. There's so much damn pressure in this work.

After about a week of not eating and running on a treadmill, I ran into Richard. We have the same agent, and he is an up-and-coming star in his own right. At 25, he walked confidence like nobody's business. He always flirted with me, but I imagined he just did that with all the girls. This day he asked me to dinner. Of course, I said no. Why would he want to go out with me?

Shortly after, I heard about Cyndi Targosz and her image lifestyle programs from another actress. Cyndi started me on a good confidence-building plan along with diet and exercise. We began to uncover the layers of my thick stubborn skin to get deep inside of the true me. Cyndi helped me realize that I did not love myself. My self-esteem and body image were almost nonexistent. There was no way, if I held on to this kind of disposition, that I could accept love, especially from a younger man.

Richard continued to pursue me. He wasn't like the other show biz types, and I liked his humorous, down-to-earth manner. It's just that I was older than he was and well, you know. When I told Cyndi about his overtures, she encouraged me to take him up on his offer for a date. After all, I was talking about him constantly, and she felt it would do me good. By now, my confidence was improving and I actually began to like myself. We clicked, and dated a short time before he proposed. We've been happily married for ten years. He makes me feel so young and beautiful! However, these days I know not to depend on looks or validation from others for my happiness. Although I confess, he sure makes it easier. I am grateful I overcame some stupid issue about being too old and not looking good enough. Age is just a number, and so is your weight."

Heather, *46*

Starting right here and now, decide to feel sexy in your own buck-naked skin. This may seem like a challenge at first, but be patient. It's not reasonable to expect a miraculous change in a poor body attitude after years of self-doubt. The first step is to stand in front of a mirror while wearing nothing. Slowly examine yourself from top to bottom. Rather than zero in on what you think are negative features, embrace the things you like about your body (nice skin, the curve of your waist, great eyes, and so on). Make an honest assessment of what you can and cannot change. It helps to try this technique after doing something that makes you feel good, like a power walk or a shower, rather than after a pity party pig-out session. Now you are ready for a makeover action plan. Set realistic goals and go for them. Daily, take ownership of your body. Delight in what is yours and yours alone.

CRUSH CRAPPY CRITICISM

Nobody likes a crappy critic. When it comes to your body image, there are two types of crappy critics to be on the lookout for. The first type falls into the category of "others," which includes family, friends, peers, and perfect strangers. With what they may claim are good intentions, they may make comments. For example, Jessica's ex-husband, Harvey, the father of her two sons, gives her butt a little whack when he picks up the kids. Then, under the guise of *kidding*, he says, "Better work on that ass, babe." It's true that her hips and derrière have spread out since she had the boys. She admits to having a little extra junk in her trunk. However, Harvey himself could use a little work, since he sports one of those middle-age male potbellies. She laughs at his words, but deep down she wants to cry. Be on the lookout for well-meaning folks being just plain mean!

The second type of crappy critic may be you, yourself, and you again. How many times have you stood in front of the mirror looking at your body as if it were on a butcher's block? Do you overscrutinize all of your parts as if to say, "look at my breasts, thighs, and hips—oh my!" Quit analyzing the parts. Look at the whole "chick" inside and out.

Now, a final word before we leave this section: just as I condemn self-criticism, I implore you not to knock down other women. It's not very flattering. Women talk about who had what done, and constantly compare themselves to others. Bashing another woman is a sure sign of your own insecurities. Besides, crappy criticism does nothing for our sisterhood. If you can't say something nice about other women, don't say anything at all!

Cyndi's Secrets™

Love yourself enough to participate in a regular exercise program that encourages you to be the best you can be. Try one of my new Cyndi's Secrets DVD workouts, fitness books or CD including:

- DVDs: *Cyndi's Secrets Love Your CURVES* (Total Body Workout), *Cyndi's Secrets Love Your ASSets* (Lower Body Workout), *Cyndi's Secrets Love Your CORE* (Abs and Back Workout), *Cyndi's Secrets BEST BUST* (Upper Body Workout).
- Books: *Ten Minute Tone-ups for Dummies, Erase Your Waist, Your Best Bust.*
- CD: *Cyndi's Secrets Drive To Fitness*

All are available at *www.starglow.com*. No more excuses!

SUPERficial Power

Once you feel confident with your inner glow, your outward appearance will automatically improve. However, it is safe to say that dating a younger guy may make you more self-conscious about your looks. This is particularly true if he is twenty years younger than you are or has a baby face. That's okay! Use the temporary insecurity as a springboard to make some really cool makeover improvements. There is a lot of power in a woman who uses both her inner and outer beauty. Outward improvements may seem superficial, but they are not. It is empowering to be the best you can be. I'll give you some of my celebrity tips throughout this program. You can find out even more Cyndi's Secrets for fashion, beauty, diet, and fitness by visiting my Web site, *www.starglow.com*. Use this information to help you unleash the goddess within you. Younger guys appreciate a woman who takes care of herself. If he doesn't—unleash him!

Boy Toy Talk

"A beautiful woman is beautiful at every age of her life. What that means is that if she's hot, she's always hot!"

Carl, 60

Spirit: Let It Move You

Using the M.B.S. System to bring out your inner goddess requires more than developing your mind and improving your body. It includes nurturing your spirit. This very crucial component can add the final layer of balance to your life. This is a very personal experience. For some it includes religious conviction, while others view it as their inner strength. It could even be a combination of the two. Your spirit is all about your attitudes, feelings, and beliefs. You can nurture your spirit by developing a positive attitude.

A positive spirit radiates energy and goodness. People—including Boy Toys—clamor to be near a happy, calm, and confident spirit. If you are a negative person by nature, you can develop a goddess spirit with practice. Be patient with yourself. Follow these guidelines:

- **Always visualize a positive result.** When you use self-talk or converse with others, see the glass half full rather than half empty. It helps to smile.
- **Goddesses are never lazy.** However, you can take time to get your nails done or get a massage. This gives your spirit a sense of rejuvenation!
- **Be aware of negative chatter in your mind.** Replace it with realistic but constructive thoughts.
- **Trust your spirit.** Sometimes things will not work out. Believe that your spirit can help you rise above anything that comes your way. Things have a way of eventually working out.
- **Use positive affirmations.** Have a talk with your inner goddess. Let the strength of your spirit help you soar through life!

Once you connect the dots that make up the M.B.S. System, much of what bugs you in life will no longer seem such a big deal. Your inner goddess light will shine brighter than ever before. Now, stay with me as we continue to prepare to be Boy Toy ready.

Chapter 5

Controlled Crying

Handling Boy Toy Struggles

Being a confident, hot BTB with an ageless spirit is a wonderful way to live. However, this does not guarantee a perfect lifetime of Boy Toy bliss. Stuff happens! With my Controlled Crying technique, you can discover how to handle struggles that are bound to occur with your Boy Toy—or any man, for that matter. Let me explain by starting with Jan's experience.

Jan and Cliff had escaped to their hideaway cabin in Aspen. They both loved to ski. With fresh powder snow on the mountain, they were ready to hit the slopes. Today was special. It marked their thirtieth wedding anniversary. The youngest of their three children was just out of college and on his own. Jan could hardly wait for this new chapter in her life. She had been dreaming of more time alone with her husband. They had been together since high school, and Cliff was her whole life. With the pressures of both of them working and raising the kids, it seemed the years just flew by. Now she was ready for things to be different.

What a delight it was to ski the slopes. She playfully licked a few flakes off his freckled face. Candlelight dinner followed at the Big Moose Lodge. Afterward, they sipped Dom Perignon Champagne near the fire. It was so cozy and in her estimation, perfect. Tucked in her suitcase was a sheer rose negligee. The kind with pink peekaboo lace strategically placed. Though they hardly made love these days, it never stopped her feelings for the man she lived for. It just wasn't that important. They were both always so busy and tired. This weekend she hoped to reignite the fires with their new freedom and commitment to their undying love. Jan was proud to have arranged it all. With a bit of a giggle she started to retreat to her boudoir to slip into something a little more comfortable.

"Wait!" Cliff proclaimed as he pulled her back to the sofa. "I have something to tell you that I know we both have been waiting for." Jan's heart was racing as she waited to hear her husband's desires. She was sure he felt just as excited as she was. With a firm yet soft voice, he whispered gently to her, "Jan, we've got to quit kidding ourselves—let's get a divorce. I'm sure you have wanted it for years, as I have. With the children all grown up, we can both have our freedom. Finally!" Jan froze at his words. Her heart was broken into tiny little pieces and shattered like glass. Though she tried to convince him to stay, he never could mend her torn soul. The damage was done and the tears flowed.

We all experience emotional distress. This eventually can lead to sadness and uncontrollable crying. Jan is not alone. Sometimes life throws us punches that seem unbearable. When I was a little girl during a disappointing situation that made me cry, my dad would pat me on the head, like only a father can do, and say to me, "Potato bug—Better days are coming!" My mother in her infinite wisdom was more of a realist. When I was upset she would say, "I'll tell you this much—life's not easy for anyone. It's hard! So pray to the good Lord and do your best." Both of these views have always helped me to cope with life's struggles. On one hand, I have hope for a better future, and on the other, I know that no matter how good the other side of the fence looks everybody has problems. Mom and Dad have helped me to develop my revolutionary concept of Controlled Crying, which I'm very excited to share with you.

As a single woman, you can pretty much count on having days that are just plain disappointing. In this chapter, you'll learn how you can use Controlled Crying to manage stress in a healthy manner. You'll discover how this emotional survival method can apply to any dating problem or struggle that may come your way. The result will transform you into a stronger woman. The confidence you will gain can help you become a better Boy Toy magnet. With Controlled Crying, you can put a bit of control back into uncontrollable situations, by allowing yourself a set amount of time to cry and act somewhat "uncontrolled." Should your dream-date Boy Toy end up being a bad-boy dud, you will have this very practical way to cope with the disappointment. Many women appreciate my Controlled Crying technique because it can sometimes allow pigging out with a healthy "little" amount of ice cream or some chocolate.

Managing Stress

Controlled Crying is an all-encompassing form of stress management. To master this technique you must develop good stress management skills. I'll help you achieve this by helping you understand the fight-or-flight response and explaining ways that you can use this to reduce your stress. This method culminates with the act of crying or allowing time for a healthy outlet of your choice. I'll show you how to use your tears (or other healthy outlet) to your advantage. Later in this chapter, I'll give you practical relaxation skills that can make it easier to cope with your problems. For once, you can shout, "For crying out loud!" and be happy about it.

The Fight-or-Flight Response

Early in the twentieth century, Harvard physiologist Walter Cannon first coined the term "fight or flight response." This response actually works in conjunction with a part of your brain called the hypothalamus. The hypothalamus releases a chemical when it is stimulated. Stress is the culprit that springs the hypothalamus into action. It doesn't matter whether the stress is from something internal, such as worrying about why your Boy Toy lied to you, or an external situation, such as an attack by a pit bull. The fight-or-flight response gets your body ready to fight or run away from either of these dogs.

During the fight-or-flight response, your body goes through some major changes. A few of the changes include an increased respiratory rate, higher adrenalin level, sharpened sight, and intensified awareness. It's amazing the way this response can protect you from bodily harm. It helps you to run before a dog bites or, in extreme cases, gives you the strength to save a child trapped under a car. We are fortunate to have this kind of response system built into our bodies. However, any kind of stress can release the chemical that puts your body in a fight-for-survival mode. This is not always beneficial. There are times when the fight-or-flight response can leave you in a quandary. For example, if your boss fires you, it is of no advantage to punch her out (fight). Running out the door serves no real purpose either (flight). So as you can see, daily pressure can create the buildup of toxic stress hormones in your body. Without a healthy outlet, they collect in your system and create havoc.

How does all this affect your love life? Well, how can you be Boy Toy ready if your body is holding stress chemicals and constantly fighting for survival? This usually ends up with a focus on fear rather than love. Is it possible that living in fear through stress is preventing you from enjoying a relationship with men—younger or older? When stress takes over your mind, it can do tremendous psychological and physical damage. Life becomes a daily crisis. Everything becomes exaggerated and it's harder to make a clear and calm decision. Have you ever started thinking about a problem during the night and magnified it ten times? Typically, the night starts with a few worries. Then the chemical released in the fight-or-flight response kicks in, causing insomnia. It can mess with the clarity of your mind as well as your body in many ways. At night, or at any time for that matter, the stress keeps building up like a time bomb. What can you do? Look at the positive side. When your body reacts to stress, it is sending you a message to take care of yourself. It's your choice to either live in a calm state or choose to be a drama queen. This is important—you can't change things that are out of your control, but you can change how you react. This is easier said than done. However, using Controlled Crying can offset the pressure building up within you. Begin by reducing your stress as much as possible, and then try your best to manage the rest.

Reducing Your Stress

The goal of the fight-or-flight response in its simplest form is survival. It may have been a lifesaver for cavemen, but nowadays it is often not a response to a life-threatening situation. Certainly, we don't want to suppress our basic instinct. With Controlled Crying, your mission is to lower the level of raging and harmful stress hormones. To reduce stress, review the environment you have created in your life. Ask yourself the following questions:

1. **Are you mentally safe?** This means that the people who know and love you protect and guard your emotions. Sometimes people who we think love us are really spirit crushers who pretend to care. Evaluate the people in your life. Quit, or at least distance yourself, from unhealthy relationships or jobs. If you don't feel great when you are with your younger man, there's a message for you. Review how you spend your time. Make it count.

2. **Are you physically safe?** If your environment is chaotic or toxic, make a change. For example, working in a smoke-filled restaurant can influence your health. You can quit your job or perhaps try to change the laws in your city. You also should be sure to stay out of harm's way, practice safe dating skills, and be alert to your physical surroundings. Always take action to protect yourself!

3. **Are you spiritually safe?** Check to see if your life has meaning and depth. This is a very personal response. Some people turn to nature to feel whole. Others look within their own soul. You can also make your own personal connection with God to ensure your spiritual sense of worth. This can help free you from the

stranglehold of guilt, shame, and all the "boo-boos" of your life. Building a strong character can have a tremendous positive effect on how you handle stress. People who are spiritually safe tend to be better at managing toxic stress levels than those who aren't.

Positive Perception

For Controlled Crying to be most effective, it pays to be a master of positive perception. Let's face it—too many things are out of your control, and you have to learn to just deal with them. Positive perception is no phony baloney; it is about living life with a great attitude! You look at what is real and shift your perception of it to a healthy direction. This is one of my best secrets to managing stress. Don't take things too personally. When a stressful event or challenge occurs, use the experience as an opportunity to grow as a person. Face up to the fact that there are things out of your control. Caving in to the toxins generated from the fight-or-flight response we talked about earlier can harm your body. Accept the things you cannot change. Believe in your heart that even if something horrible happens to you, you will emerge better because of it.

Boy Toy Talk

"I thought my life was over when Cliff left me after thirty years of marriage. Somehow, I started living again. At 70, I met 55-year-old Rob at a weekend seminar. He makes me feel sexy and he's fun. We've been together for two years and we're still going strong. The thought of growing old with Cliff seems so boring compared to being with Rob!"

Jan, 72 (whose story was featured at the start of this chapter)

Crying on Command: Healthy Outlets

To manage stress you have to figure out a healthy way to free your body of the toxic stress hormones that bombard you daily. For years, I have given seminars on this topic. However, there have been times when I couldn't live up to the constant calm I knew would be healthy for me. During an immediate or sudden high-stress occurrence, I found that some of the practical stress-management solutions, such as yoga or meditation, were limiting. I still applaud, rave about, and practice traditional stress-management skills, so please don't think I am putting these down. I highly recommend them. It's just that there are times when these skills are unrealistic. Say you are dating a younger man who has just arrived two hours late for the third date in a row. Sitting in a yoga position chanting "Ommmmmm" as he walks in the door may not be your most effective solution. Asking him to leave and telling him never to come back as you shut the door behind him may be much more effective and healthier for you.

What sets my Controlled Crying program apart from other stress-management programs is that you now can *give yourself permission* to cry or use another healthy outlet to get over the initial hump of the stress. Cry a few tears, scream (don't attack), or eat a *little* ice cream. It feels damn good and even serves as a catharsis! Stay in this mode for only a short period of time, lest you cross over into an unhealthy zone. Never do anything that would hurt you or another person.

Use common sense when deciding how long to stay in a Controlled Crying mode. Certainly, if you are grieving after losing a loved one, you will need more time. That's perfectly acceptable. Wearing the same jogging suit and skipping showers for a week after a jerk stands you up is stretching my concept a little too far. Get the picture?

Cyndi's Secrets™

> Keeping tears bottled up can be unhealthy. If you are so upset you can't cry, try this technique from my acting training. Stare at a light without blinking as you recall your sad or angry issue. Sit by an open window as you stare. Imagine tears rolling down your face as you yawn. Almost instantly real teardrops usually appear. Just get it out.

To further clarify Controlled Crying: When an occasional high-stress situation occurs, use tears, a scream, a *tiny* portion of chocolate, or your favorite temporary outlet. Then daily, incorporate stress-management skills such as deep breathing, meditation, and exercise into your life. Practicing these skills daily will carry you through the extra-tough times. It is the combination of daily skills coupled with your ability to give yourself permission to cry that spells stress-management success!

Following are a few stress-management skills you can use to ward off toxic stress chemicals:

- **Deep Breathing:** Use slow, deep breaths that originate from your diaphragm, not from your chest. As a trained speech pathologist, I can't stress the importance of this enough. Do this daily and during high-stress situations, such as while crying or screaming. Make deep breathing second nature and notice the incredible health benefits.
- **Progressive Muscle Relaxation:** While working with people who stutter, I found that progressive muscle relaxation not only cured their speech impediment but also did wonders for managing stress. I've been using this skill ever since. It consists of alternating muscle contractions followed by relaxation. Do this

with one muscle group at a time. For example, start with your face. Scrunch it tight for 30 seconds. Take a deep breath and release your muscles. Next, contract the neck muscles and then release. Follow this progression from head to toe.

- **Exercise:** Come on—you know this one. When you exercise, you feel better. There's tons of research to prove it. Besides, it's a great way to look hot too!
- **Prayer:** Prayer can provide a healthy outlet that allows you to remove some of the burdens of life from your shoulders. It's a beautiful and naturally healing way to remove toxic stress chemicals from your body.
- **Meditation:** Meditation brings you into the present moment. The goal is to quiet your mind of chatter, which in itself is beneficial for stress management.
- **Hydrotherapy:** Who can argue the benefits of a warm bath or Jacuzzi? It increases the circulation and calms the soul. Add aromatherapy candles to enhance your pleasure.

These are just a few of the many healthy outlets available. Discover what works for you. Try yoga, massage therapy, perhaps painting or another way to express your emotions. Controlled Crying won't solve all your problems, but it can help you cope, and like my mother says, "Nobody's got it easy!"

Chapter 6

Boy Toy Hangouts

Start in Your Heart

By now, you know how to embrace your ageless spirit and realize that true beauty and confidence come from within. You even have the tools to use my Controlled Crying technique to help you get through any Boy Toy mishap. Carry that empowering attitude with you as you search for Boy Toys. Don't be surprised by the opportunities that might come your way. Let me share a little personal story with you:

> It was a warm spring evening when I sped through the canyon in my red sports car, top down and hair blowing in the wind. I was heading into the Hollywood Hills to one of my favorite writing places—the outside patio of a charming grocery store in the mountains, complete with cappuccino and free wireless access. My mission was to finish this segment of the book on where and how to meet Boy Toys. I was energized and felt ready to pen my thoughts and share my words of wisdom. My laptop hung over my shoulder in its pretty pink carrying case as I lugged a huge canvas tote filled with all the working-girl essentials: PDA, research notes, bottled water,

Bluetooth cell phone, and lipstick. Very focused and definitely driven—I was ready!

However, after staring at a blank word-processing document for nearly half an hour, I did the unthinkable. I somehow deleted my entire toolbar. Help!

Oh well! I did what a girl's got to do. I asked a young hunk coming out of the store for help. Let me assure you I was so desperate to get my computer working I was not thinking Boy Toy potential at the time. Well, he didn't know how to solve the problem and enlisted another guy for help, which created a stir. Before long there were four Boy Toys buzzing like bees around me. They were competing with a frenzy to solve the computer problem. Finally, Brad right-clicked this and then he left-clicked that and selected something or other. He eventually saved the day and gave me his phone number for a future connection. Whether I responded or not doesn't matter. A new Boy Toy option was available. I should say that Boy Toy options (plural) were available, since the Boy Toys who did not save the day seemed pretty cool too!

It is so easy to go through life trying to chart out where we can meet guys, scheming with our friends some sort of Boy Toy–trap strategy. And yes, in this chapter I'll give you tons of tips as to where you can find Boy Toys. However, to really learn where the Boy Toys are, you have to start in your heart. At that grocery store in the mountains I experienced firsthand the value of being willing to put yourself out there every single day. It starts with an energy within your heart and a willingness to share kindness with all others—men, women, children, and of course little doggies. Sometimes, it's not being afraid to show a touch of vulnerability. I felt sort of stupid about messing up the computer, but truthfully, people need people. I am not talking about playing dumb;

it's just that by keeping an open heart and mind, you can remove blinders that limit your Boy Toy–seeking potential.

Cyndi's Secrets™

The feminist movement has done wonders for women. Bravo! However, as women, there are times we try to be all things to all people. It is okay to admit that you cannot be all things at all times. I'm not as computer-savvy as I'd like to be, but you know what? I'm getting better every day. A good Boy Toy will appreciate both your strengths and weaknesses.

Go Back to School

There is no better Boy Toy playground than the one at school. Taking an adult education class provides an excellent opportunity to meet a lot of guys in a very safe environment. On top of that, you already know you have the same or similar interests. Go ahead and pick up that catalog from the local college or adult education classes. Take a cooking class, art history, or try to learn hip-hop. Perhaps it's even time for you to make good on that promise you made years ago to go back and finish your high school diploma, or the degree you forgot about when your first child arrived out of wedlock and your youth escaped with a burping beep. Boy Toy or not, you deserve to keep increasing your knowledge base for a well-rounded life.

Meeting people in a class is very casual. If you are shy, you don't have to worry about having to go out on a "date." Start by going out with a group. Then you can offer to help a potential Boy Toy study, or ask him to help you. If he isn't interested, it is an easy, nonthreatening split. Who knows? He just may want to delve deeper into the course of life with you.

Boy Toy Talk

At 29, Fred was studying to be a priest. Something within prevented him from following through with his ordination plans, and he asked to take a year off to go on sabbatical. After much prayer and meditation, Fred decided it was time to return and complete his theological studies. It was his very first day returning to class when "she" walked into the room. Fred melted at the very sight of her. In an instant, something told him that she was the one. Martha was there to study Pastoral Ministry. She was sixteen years his senior, but you never would have guessed it. In fact, he had no idea that her age was 45 when he met her. He never cared. He is adamant till this day that age is not an issue. Fred and Martha have been happily married for 29 years. Fred is now 58 and Martha is 74.

Good Deeds May Fill Your Needs

By doing good for yourself and others you pave the way for a tremendous amount of self-worth, which is something Boy Toys find hot. Compared to older men, younger men exhibit a tremendous amount of appreciation for good deeds done by a woman. They admire it, while their older counterparts all too frequently expect it. Volunteer for charity events, political campaigns, and fundraisers.

Let your spirit continue to guide you as you find these special guys at your church, synagogue, or wherever you may worship. I know a gorgeous Boy Toy who studies with a faith group once a week. This gem told me that even if he were younger, he would take an attractive woman who had depth of character any day over a young sexy body with nothing going on upstairs. Amen!

Planes, Trains, and Automobiles

It's a small, small world, and I'm not talking about a children's ride at Disneyland. Nowadays people are constantly in motion. Hardly a day goes by that most of us don't use some form of transportation. Travel stations are a perfect place for a hot Boy Toy Babe like you to take action. My friend Crystal commutes regularly between San Francisco and Los Angeles. One time she connected so well with a handsome, sophisticated gent in the curbside baggage check-in line that the skycap accidentally checked her luggage on his plane. It was so pure and innocent that she remembers it like it was yesterday. They both let their guards down and just had a great time giggling like kids as they walked into the airport, neither one of them wanting to part. She was charmed as he nervously walked into the ladies' room by mistake and then tripped on his own feet, all shook up with embarrassment. Everybody just assumed these two were together. They exchanged numbers, and for several months had a brief, hot, heavy romantic interlude. Okay, they didn't end up walking down the aisle together, but till this day, they remain the best of friends. Remember to embrace each experience for what it is. Have fun with where you are in life. If it doesn't work out perfectly—simply catch another flight!

Take advantage of your everyday travels. Strike up a conversation with a hot young guy during a delay at the airport. Ask the friendly chap on the subway whether the seat next to him is taken. You can discover a lot in long ticket lines, magazine shops, and other in-transit locations. Boy Toys are particularly mobile. In general, they travel with less baggage than the older guys, who may travel with steamer trunks . . . and run out of steam!

Boy Toy Hot Spots

One of my goals is to help you expand your personal menu of men. Please do not think I mean for you to ignore all older men. In fact, I have always considered myself an equal opportunity dater. However, Boy Toys can provide a welcome and empowering change to your life, and fess up—they often offer a fresh feast for sore eyes. You now have more men to choose from, and girlfriend, it's all about choice! Following are some great Boy Toy hangouts:

Cyndi's Secrets™

Don't be afraid to let family and friends know that you are open-minded about dating a younger guy. If you are shy about admitting this, simply let them know you are in the market for a guy who is not set in his ways. They will get the picture pronto! You can admit to looking for a guy who is active and takes really good care of himself. If a Boy Toy Babe is going to stay hot, her man had better be his personal best too.

- **Cybercafés:** These little wireless hot zones are a great place to get connected. When you spot a Boy Toy target, be sure you check to see if he has a wedding band on his finger. If not, take a deep breath and proceed with caution. If there's an empty seat next to him, you are at a great advantage. Politely ask him if someone else is using the empty seat. Pay attention to his reaction to you. If he seems the slightest interested, you can slide into the seat on the side that is closest to him without invading his space. Be sure to smile and make eye contact with him. This serves as a subliminal cue that you are interested. See if he reciprocates your small talk. If he doesn't, back off lest you come across like a desperate cougar.

- **Hardware stores:** Boy Toys love these places! Try Saturday morning or afternoon, when many come out to start weekend projects. What a nice benefit to find a guy who also is a handyman. Nowadays many women are quite adept at handy work. If you are, you can help him, or at least share a mutual interest. This is one time when you can be happy about throwing a wrench in your relationship.

- **Public places:** Grocery stores, restaurants, Laundromats, bookstores, and any everyday place where people congregate can be a potential meeting ground. It helps to be prepared with plenty of small talk. For example, while at the grocery store you can say, "Gee—I always get in the wrong checkout line." This gives you a chance to chat up the young Boy Toy in front of you.

- **The car wash:** It has been said that a man's car is an extension of his penis. Well, I don't know if that is true, but I do know that on Friday at lunch or on the way home from work you can find lots of Boy Toys getting their wheels ready for the weekend. You can discover a lot about a man while waiting for your car. Of course, you shouldn't judge a man by the car he drives, but confess—you do check it out, if only to know his personality better. Besides, they love to talk about their cars. Is he sporty? Is he a classic? Is he practical? Does he care about saving the environment, or is he hanging on to a hooptie? If you want to approach a potential Boy Toy simply ask him, "What year is your car?" Most likely, you don't have to say another thing. Many Boy Toys will expound on how their penis extension zips around curves. They'll brag about the mileage that they have, or how they are just "breaking her in." Realize that you probably will only see the exterior at this meeting. If sparks fly, his interior thoughts can be detailed later.

- **Billiard rooms:** If you haven't stepped into a billiard room in a while, now is a good time. Boy Toys love this sport and welcome women—especially hot BTBs! Helpful instruction from the younger guy at the next table can lead to a close encounter. Of course, if pool is your strength he may appreciate a lesson from you as well, as you teach him how to put the proper ball in the corner pocket.

Chapter 7

Friendly Flirting Made Easy

Flirting: Your Natural Instinct

Legendary 1930s film actress Mae West was famous in her day for bawdy, flirtatious lines including, "Hey there, big boy!" and "Why don't you come up and see me sometime?" She was way ahead of her time and one of the finest Boy Toy Babes to boot! Miss West had a Coke-bottle figure and embraced her curvy beautiful body and sensuality. She had all this in a ballsy, powerful package that was only five feet tall. When she spotted a younger conquest, she was not shy about going after him. With a slow, staccato, seductive drawl, she would murmur, "Is that a gun in your pocket or are you just glad to see me?" These days gun control laws are tighter, but modern men still carry that same pistol in their pockets. Anthropological research shows that flirting often leads to lots of pocket pistols—if you know what I mean. This is part of our natural instinct. In fact if we did not flirt and attract the opposite sex, our reproductive genes would die and so would all of humanity. Perhaps that's how the Wild West was won—the Wild Miss West, that is!

Many evolutionary psychologists believe that flirting is the foundation of our entire civilization. They conclude that our brain, which includes our IQ, speech and language skills, and everything that separates us from animals, is nothing more than an instrument to attract and hold on to the opposite sex. They argue that everything we achieve and become in life is secondary to and a result of flirting. Well, I don't know if I agree with this 100 percent. However, who can argue with the tons of scientific research done that says flirting is part of our natural instinct. We need to do it for survival, and gosh darn, it is fun!

Flirting Etiquette

Well now, sister, hold your panties up. When it comes to flirting, there are certain rules of etiquette one must follow in society. This is particularly true with younger men. Let's show a little class. There are many unspoken guidelines that tell us when, where, how, and with whom we can flirt. Generally, we follow these guidelines without even thinking about it.

There are times when even a Boy Toy Babe at her best must refrain from outward overtures to the opposite sex. For example, flirtatiously chatting up your boss's son at her funeral is not appropriate, ever. Okay, that's a bit extreme, but you get the picture. I am also appalled by the number of women these days who find it good sport to flirt with another woman's boyfriend or even worse, another woman's husband. Can we please stop this competitive nonsense among ourselves?

Research shows that men frequently misread the friendliness of women. Some guys equate a woman's warm smile with a hot tub and a rub. Hence they think, "She wants me." Of course, the woman may just be—well, friendly. This is particularly a problem if you are a playful personality. Being bubbly myself, I have learned to be careful not to send the wrong signals. Does this mean I hide my giggles and wear only turtlenecks? Heck no! I love people and delight in celebrating life with both the men and the women whom I encounter daily. There is a huge difference in flirting out of the joy for life versus the sexual play used when capturing the attention of a younger man. However, they both feed off each other and can work together well. In this chapter, we will discuss how you can use flirting in a healthy way to attract a younger man. You can also use this information to make sure Mr. Hot Tub and a Rub reads you correctly. If he still thinks you are hot for him, feel free to use moves from your kickboxing class while wearing stilettos.

Cyndi's Secrets™

Ladies—if another woman flirts with your man and he responds inappropriately, do not take it out on the woman. This only feeds the ego of your man and makes you look bad. Besides, many men actually enjoy a catfight at your expense. Opt to approach him about his actions. Shouldn't he be on your team? As a couple, you can't control outside forces. Together you can combat problems and "comfort" each other. He should protect you in this situation. Likewise, if another man flirts inappropriately with you, it is very sexy to turn and plant a kiss on your guy. Comfort each other.

The Looks Factor

Consider the attractiveness of a potential Boy Toy target, or any man for that matter, when determining who you are going to flirt with. It's not that I would expect you to flirt with a guy you don't think is hot. However, research says that relationships in which the partners are equal in the looks department have a better chance at succeeding. Do not let that statement steer you away from attempting to hook up with a younger guy. Equal looks does not have anything to do with the fact that you may have a few wrinkles. A younger man is usually looking at the whole package and sees you as being worldly, experienced, and extremely sexy. Don't forget that internal beauty and handsomeness is powerful as well.

Other studies also show that 80 percent of women believe they are too fat. Most women try to achieve a size that is two sizes smaller than what men find hot. What does this mean to you? Chances are you are better looking than you think. Hey—how 'bout looking for a better-looking guy than you normally would? Why not expand your dating options and start including Boy Toys? Brilliant!

Boy Toy Talk

"Every morning like clockwork, Carolyn would stroll into the deli at 7:30 sharp. I usually was there first since I work the early shift at the firehouse. This went on for weeks. I couldn't keep my eyes off of her but feared she would think I was some sort of weirdo. Tall and obviously successful—I couldn't imagine this vision of grace and sophistication ever taking notice of me. She made me weak at the knees. Thankfully, she asked me for directions to a local office building one morning. She followed me behind my fire truck. This gave me the courage to ask her out. Wow! She said yes!"

Eduardo, 39 (Carolyn is 51)

Flirting with Disaster

Flirting can sometimes be disastrous. If you approach a Boy Toy target and find that he is sending signals that say "back off," then do just that—back off! Never place yourself in a position where you are the female counterpart to Mr. Hot Tub. It is very disturbing when an older woman takes on the role of a pushy predator. Suddenly a hot Boy Toy Babe looks more like a cranky old cougar and a not very attractive one at that. Don't do it!

How to Make Your Move

You don't have to look like a Greek goddess to flirt with flying colors. It just takes a little spunk and some basic friendly flirting techniques. It may surprise you to know that when you meet a man, his first impression of you is based 55 percent on your appearance and body language, 38 percent on the manner in which you speak, and only 7 percent on what you say. This bit of knowledge can serve you well. Considering that most woman lose sleep trying to think of what they can "say" to a potential mate, it might be better to work on improving your body language and nonverbal skills. So get your beauty rest.

Nonverbal Flirting

Following are a few nonverbal flirting techniques. Be warned that these moves are very powerful. Use with caution!

THE EYES HAVE IT

When approaching a younger man, the first tool of the Boy Toy trade is to give him the "look." The look that catches his attention with a glance lasts a little over a second. Too much longer than that and he may think you are creepy. If he reciprocates the "look," there is a good chance that he might be interested. Should there be no eye connection, it's a safe bet that he's not interested (or he could be blind). This information can save you from a hurtful or embarrassing situation.

To help you avoid missing any glances coming your way from potential suitors, wear your glasses if you need them. I used to leave my glasses in the car when approaching my destination—it was the old vanity excuse. One day, a cute young hunk mustered up the courage to approach me for a date. He had been making eyes at me during lunch from afar for a couple years but I never responded. He assumed that I wasn't interested. Heck—I never even saw him. We had a wonderful relationship that lasted a year and are still good friends. Now I wear contacts when I want to make contacts!

Cyndi's Secrets™

I must confess that I have entered "private space" during some first meetings. Although this is usually not recommended, it can work when you are absolutely sure that a Boy Toy is interested in you. The sexy secret is to enter his zone quickly and then exit out before he even knows what hit him. It should almost seem like an accident. Younger men go crazy over this move. It's a playful, healthy tease! Again, be absolutely sure that he is interested.

BEING SPACEY

To successfully flirt, I highly recommend that you be "spacey"—but in this case that does not mean you should act like a ditz. It relates to the distance or space you keep from someone you have just met. Perhaps even more important is observing the distance the person keeps from you. It's like this: if eye contact is successful, move in up to four feet from your target. Should your Boy Toy be responding positively, you can move in another foot or two closer to him. Never get closer than a foot and a half away. Closer than eighteen inches and you are entering "private space," which is usually reserved for lovers and close family and friends. Being spacey helps you to avoid embarrassment. You have the opportunity to bolt quickly should he not respond to your advances. Respect his space.

BODY TALK

When flirting with a potential mate, your body is saying more than you probably realize. You can also study what your Boy Toy target is saying by watching his stance. Either of you could be lying when you talk, but your bodies are often unknowingly spilling the beans. For example, he may be speaking to you, but only his head is in your direction while the rest of his body is toward the door. Honey—this guy wants to zip out. Be a smart Boy Toy Babe and dart first. On a positive note, if he is unconsciously imitating your actions, such as adopting your posture, there is a good chance he is interested. Psychologists call this behavior "posture mirroring." You could reciprocate by tilting your head and nodding with affirmation or clasping your hands in appreciation. Gestures, posture, facial expressions, and even the sound of your voice all contribute to the messages you are sending and receiving.

When it comes to body talk, the action of touch is touchy. Be cautious. Using touch inappropriately may make a younger man assume you want sex. Of course, if you *are* extending a purely sexual invitation, using touch could work, but only after you are certain he feels the same way. This is not to say that you can't use touch when initiating friendly flirting. Touching the arm, back, or even the shoulder of a Boy Toy can be a safe and often welcome gesture. Once again, if he does not respond—back off.

Welcoming Words

When it comes to verbal flirting, the studies say that women have got it over the guys. Of course, that is no surprise; just think how many men hate talking on the phone. The good news is that younger guys are in many ways more adept at conversation than their older counterparts. Their mothers have raised them with the concept of feminism and the importance of expressing feelings and being sensitive. This is not to say that Boy Toys do not have their share of "beer commercial moments," where women are nothing more than a *yada yada* in the background.

Even if your potential Boy Toy is in touch with his feelings, do not be surprised if your first meeting leaves him tongue-tied. Take the risk and make the first move. Verbal flirting in the form of opening lines does not need to make your stomach queasy. Rather than trying to come up with some phony repartee, choose to talk about the usual stuff. You know—the weather, or how he knows the bride at a wedding you're both attending. Just be you! Needless to say, all of us can benefit from improving our communication skills, both speaking and listening. Try joining a group such as Toastmasters International (*www.toastmasters.org*) to improve your communication skills. Besides, you never know who you might meet.

The Secret Code: Young-Guy Speak

Dude! Heyyyyyy! Flirting with younger men does not mean you have to start using terms such as these. We all know how ridiculous older men can look when they date younger women and rather than stay true to themselves, they adopt a pathetic midlife trying-to-seem-younger demeanor coupled with an ear-to-ear bad comb-over haircut. Let's learn from their mistakes. Always be true to you.

Being aware of language differences and understanding young-guy speak can help you tremendously when flirting with a Boy Toy. For example, when a young guy is speaking about the future, he usually is not looking far in advance. If he says, "let's make a plan," he means for the weekend, not for life. Younger people generally speak more about the "now." If you are talking about ten years from now, be sure to say, "*ten years* from now."

Many Boy Toys are afraid to make a move on a hot BTB. Young-guy-speak romantic overtures sent your way may be less obvious than those of an older man. That's because when a younger guy sees you, he is probably imagining you with tons of older and more powerful men swarming around you. Younger men sometimes wonder why someone as special as you would desire them. They see you as sophisticated and worldly. That can be intimidating. (Hey—I'm not making this up. Guys in my survey really feel this way!) The big secret is that a younger man is still the man, and he wants to feel as such. You need to show him the way, but let him make the first move. Oh, I know that many women ask guys out these days, and that can be a turn-on. However, the guys in my survey preferred a woman actively express-ing an interest that allowed them to make the move. That means you need to pay attention to their guy speak and then give them some sort of a signal that you are interested. For example, Jason was too shy to approach Carol. When he said to her, "I have to find someone to test my new recipes out for chef school," he was really using young-guy speak to ask her out. Carol quickly offered to be his guinea pig. Now he cooks regularly for her and her two children. Another safe young-guy-speak approach is to ask him to "join" you for something such as coffee or a walk with your dogs. This is not intimidating, and opens the door for future dates should the two of you click.

Following are some examples of young-guy speak. These are things that a young guy may say, followed by what he really means.

Young-Guy Speak	The Secret Code
My car is in the shop.	I don't own a car.
I prefer quiet neighborhood restaurants.	I can't afford the expensive restaurants that you usually go to.
I give a great massage!	Do you want to have sex? (old and young use this line)
Meet me at MySpace.	He wants you to join his online community – not a reference to his apartment.
Shortie	Term for girlfriend
I just got back from the gym.	Did you see my pecs?
The Big "O"	He's not referring to Oprah.

Flirting Signals Cheat Sheet

To help you understand flirting a little better, I have prepared the Flirting Signals Cheat Sheet. Use this valuable tool to help you understand flirting.

FEMALE FLIRTING SIGNS

- Showing off your neck and inner wrists
- Tossing your hair or twirling it playfully
- Diminutive moves; attempting to appear smaller (this is where the female exhibits playful coyness by shrinking her shoulders inward)
- Sticking the breasts and butt out

MALE FLIRTING SIGNS

- Gut sucked in and chest puffed out
- Straightening the hair as if to preen
- Stretching as if to say in a manly way, "How 'bout those Lions!"
- Holding on to a belt, or belt buckle

MALE AND FEMALE FLIRTING SIGNS

- Eye contact
- Posture mirroring
- "Accidentally on purpose" touching

Chapter 8

Make the Connection

High-Tech Dating Talk

It was 1998 when pop-culture filmgoers became familiar with the phrase "you've got mail" in the movie of the same name. The movie depicted two lead characters who established a romantic relationship over the Internet before they actually met in person. It was only a novelty at the time, but boy, have times changed. Like it or not, high-tech dating is at an all-time high. Technology has introduced us to text messaging, love match sites, and cell phone dating. I've even seen restaurants designed with computer screens at each table. This allows you to flirt or send a safe cyberwink to the hunk five tables over in between courses. According to a study conducted by the Online Publishers Association (OPA) and comScore Networks, in one year U.S. residents spent almost a half billion dollars in online dating and personals. Whew! In fact, the Nielsen/NetRatings, which is the leader in Internet research, recently announced its online dating survey results. They conclude that one in three Internet users would now use the Web to meet a potential dating partner. They also stated that the Internet is the third most-popular method for getting a date. Meeting mates through friends and at bars or clubs were ranked at number one and two, respectively.

I doubt that high-tech dating is going to negate the traditional charm of meeting a guy the old-fashioned way. However, more and more hookups are happening online. Let me help you sort out the pros and cons of online dating, so you can decide whether attempting to make a match on the Web is right for you. One thing that is certain is that younger guys are more comfortable with the Internet than are older men, and it is safe to say that many Boy Toys may be perusing the dating sites. In this chapter, I offer practical advice for online dating. You'll also discover other dating services and valuable information on dating safely. Use the information to help you delete the creeps and bookmark your favorites. If you choose, you can be a dating cyberspace sensation.

Becoming a Cyberspace Sensation

There are numerous dating sites on the Internet. You can even find them for niche groups targeting race, religion, or your favorite hobby. Many specify what type of relationship you are looking for, ranging from casual friend to just sex and on to dating and/or marriage. Be aware that online dating is a business. Some may offer a free introductory peek through the site, but usually then command a fee—for example, $24.95 a month. If you sign up for several months in advance, you can get a discount. Many sites require that you pay an additional fee if you want to contact a potential mate. Legally you would have to agree to the Terms of Use to understand the rules, pricing, and of course confidentiality. These issues vary from site to site.

Whether they are worth the effort and expense or not is the great debate of this century. Certainly, many couples have met on the Net. Modern-day psychologists are eager to study the long-term effects of online matchmaking. There are also plenty of horror stories to be told. When it comes to love and dating, whether you first meet on the Web or in person, there are no guarantees. Perhaps that is the real lesson—dating in any circumstance comes with its share of duds and delights. You choose the format that works for you. You might fear that you are too old to attract a younger guy on the Web. The reality is that there are tons of younger men looking for a match, and they do not care about age. Some are looking for serious relationships, while others just want to play. To succeed on the Web, you need to be honest about what sort of hookup you desire. Finding someone to be honest with you can be the real battle. Roberta never expected the flood of "young meat," as she calls her Boy Toys, to inundate her e-inbox. Then there is Jessica. She met Blade on the Net. He is ten years younger than she is, and they have scored happily at love. They've been monogamous for almost a year and enjoy a happy, healthy, fulfilling relationship.

Boy Toy Talk

"I'm 58, extremely successful and happy being single. The Internet seemed like something I could dabble in but I never really expected much—especially a younger guy. It was astonishing to me when I suddenly got all these e-mails from younger guys asking me out. Boy Toys totally turn me on. There was one young guy who was persistent. I didn't respond for the longest time because he was only 28. Well, that seemed too young even for someone as liberal as I am. But honey—this guy did more to make me look and feel younger than my face lift, boob job, and Botox treatments did combined. I've got to tell you I knew it was temporary, but I didn't care. We both knew the game. My Boy Toy was just the boost I needed."

Roberta, 58

The Good, the Bad, and Sometimes Ugly

Searching for a Boy Toy online comes with its share of pros and cons. Following are a few reasons some people enjoy cyberdating:

- **Instant gratification:** With e-mail, instant messaging, and private chatrooms you can quickly get immediate attention. It's not always good, but it is immediate.
- **No pressure:** The Internet gives you the freedom to control with whom you want to connect. Most sites make it very simple to block unwanted e-mails.
- **Develops substance:** Couples that relate via the Internet often chat on a deep level before meeting each other.
- **Determines articulation:** Dating online gives you a chance to improve your writing and verbal skills. It also provides an opportunity to evaluate how articulate your potential partner may be.
- **Provides a large sea of men:** There is no shortage of guys to choose from on these Web sites, though catching the right one may take a lot of fishing.

Cyberdating also comes complete with its share of cons and con artists. Following are a few of the negatives to Internet dating. Buyer beware!

- **Lack of honesty:** The Internet is laden with liars, cheaters, predators, and every other scumbag of society. You cannot trust somebody you just met on a Web site or believe everything he says. He may not even be who he says he is. Always meet in a public place during the daytime. It's a good idea to bring your friend

Bruno and a pit bull too. Well, that may be a little extreme—I'm just saying be cautious and be safe!

- **Your truth:** Okay ladies—let's be fair. It's important that you are truthful too. Certainly if you fudge about a couple of pounds, it is not a big deal. However, should you finally hook up and you have lied about something important, it could cause a lot of drama. Take my friend Chad. He belongs to an online matchmaker site and enjoys dating women of all ages. Chad figures that it is a woman's right to knock off a few years from her age on the site. However, when he met his cyberdate for coffee, he was not happy that she had used her daughter's photo instead of her own in the profile.

- **False love:** Be careful not to fall in love with false love. At 3:00 A.M., alone on a Saturday night, it is very easy to develop a need for companionship. Be clear on the difference between cybersex and late-night erotica versus real love. The Internet can never replace the touch of someone who really cares about you.

- **Safety:** For many reasons, the Internet is not always the safest place to find a date. However, if you exercise caution, just as you would on any date, you can proceed. I'll discuss this in more detail later in this chapter.

The Acronym Act

Acronyms have become a big part of our culture. Blame it on text messaging, the Web or whatever; Boy Toys are using them nonstop. To help you communicate a little bit better with him I've provided a list of the most popular acronyms hitting inboxes everywhere:

LOL: Laugh Out Loud   **CBL:** Come Back Later
GTG: Got to Go   **BF:** Boyfriend
GF: Girlfriend   **L8R:** Later
JAM: Just a minute   **BTW:** By the Way
TX: Thanks   **GMAB:** Give Me a Break
AFK: Away from Keyboard   **BWK:** Big Wet Kiss

Following are a few new ones that I created in honor of all Boy Toy Babes on the planet. Feel free to use these with pride!

BT: Boy Toy   **MBT:** My Boy Toy
BTB: Boy Toy Babe   **MBTBO:** My Boy Toy, Back Off!
BTM: Boy Toy Mom   **BTD:** Boy Toy Dad

Dating Sites

There are numerous dating sites available. In fact, they keep popping up every day. Some of the more popular ones include *www.match.com*, *www.eharmony.com*, *www.American Singles.com*, and *www.Date.com*. One site, *www.agematch.com*, claims to be the number-one site for women dating younger men. It's up to you to take your time perusing the Web to discover which site, if any, is best for you. To help you with your options, visit *www.datingsitesreviews.com* for reviews and ratings of numerous dating sites. This can help you from getting lost in cyberspace!

Cell Phone Dating

If you enjoy standard online dating, you'd better not get too comfortable. High-tech wired sources say that cell dating or mobile dating, as it is also called, is the next big thing. With cell phone dating you can chat, text, meet, and greet through your phone. This provides another opportunity to hook up with more Boy Toys. Many younger men totally get into this digital stuff. Even if you never use this approach, the Boy Toys in your life will be dually impressed that you are not only sexy and smart, but cybersavvy. You don't have to tell them I gave you this tidbit. It's our secret. Shhhhhh!

This is how it works. You put together a short bio or profile that is digitally stored in your phone as a "dating ID." This then allows you to check out other IDs online or by calling a phone number supplied by your service. For now these sites are often free, but standard text-messaging rates apply. A little catch—there's also usually a small dating service fee per message. Some people fear getting electronically harassed, but not enough to stop the trend.

Most cell dating Web sites home in on subscribers who are in the same area or nearby location. The focus is more on a small community to encourage actual meeting opportunities. Some companies even install "homing devices" utilizing Bluetooth technology that signal you when another "dating ID" user is within thirty feet of you. This can be particularly useful at bars, clubs, and at the mall. The trendsetters call it *proximity dating.* It's already the rage in some countries in Europe and Asia. So girlfriend, grab your handset. Keep your Boy Toys in the palm of your hand!

Dating Services: The Nuts and Bolts

So far, we've discussed many different ways to meet younger guys. It should be apparent to you by now that my Boy Toy Program is all about making choices. You're your own Boy Toy Babe boss! Another way to explore even more options is through dating services. Let me offer some tips should you want to go this route. There are dating services that organize parties, social functions, and events. Some include question-naires, private interviews, photographs, or video profiles. Some are open to the general public, while others specialize in niche groups. Dating services can run the gamut from being listed on Craigslist.org to paying top dollar for a high-end matchmaker. Before you spend your money or invest your emotions in a dating service, consider the following:

- What makes the service special? Most dating services cater to individuals' dating desires. For example, some specialize in casual dating while others are for people who are more marriage minded. Are you interested in companionship, dating only younger guys, or open to a wider range? Ask whether the service can meet your specific needs.
- Do you like the personnel? Make sure that you can personally relate to a company contact, or even several contacts at the service. This can help you get insider tips about everything from upcoming social events to thoughts about your hair. It can make your entire experience more enjoyable.
- Be intuitive. If you don't feel good about spending your money with an organization, don't!
- Understand the costs. Make sure that you understand what you are going to pay and what you get for your money.
- Make sure that the dating service respects your privacy. Ask if they sell your contact information. That is, unless you want an e-mail inbox and postal address swamped with lonely-hearts junk mail.
- Read all rules and regulations and any contract you sign.

Matchmaker, Make Me a Match!

Matchmaking has been around forever. It conjures up the image of a little old lady trying to pair off her granddaughter with a neighbor's son. However, in the modern world of dating services, the professional matchmaker is highly specialized. He or she is usually ready to provide the ultimate in individual and personal service. Most pride themselves on quality rather than quantity. They usually spend a lot of time interviewing and getting to know you. The purpose is to find out as much about you as possible. They quiz you to find out exactly what you are looking for in a potential mate. Many do extensive background checks to ensure the quality of their members. Sometimes the service includes helping you with a makeover. They consult with you about hair, makeup, and the clothes you wear. They tell you what they think will make you look your best. Sort of like what most of our moms would try to do when we girls were in high school—except with matchmakers, you might actually listen and even "obey."

Having a matchmaker help you can cost from about $1,000 on up, making it one of the most expensive forms of dating services. One exclusive Beverly Hills agency I talked with told me it generally charges from $6,000 to $15,000 dollars for its service. I thanked the representative and went on to explain that my readers looking for younger men would be happy to know this. He quickly interrupted me. Women, he announced, are charged approximately $25,000 when looking for a younger man. He considered this *special research*. Hmmmmmmm! That's approximately 40 percent more than what he charges an older man looking for a younger woman. Forty percent more—well, isn't that *special!* Yet women on average make 23 percent less than men do. That just does not seem fair.

This does not mean that all matchmakers are sexist or that they discriminate. In fact, many provide a great service to successful women who have money and don't have time to go out looking for a specific type of man. Just be sure you take the time to do your homework. Should you choose to use a matchmaker, be sure to ask several questions, including how much a guy gets charged for the same service. Many of these agencies have room to negotiate. It is interesting to note that most of the matchmakers I spoke with proclaimed a steady increase in the number of women signing up with the intention of finding a younger man. It's obvious that as women become more independent, they naturally become pickier in the man department, and Boy Toys become more appealing.

Speed Dating

Speed dating is a popular matchmaking process. The goal is to meet a large number of potential dates. Rabbi Yaacov Deyo of Aish HaTorah originated it. You read right—a rabbi! He wanted to help Jewish singles meet with the motive of getting married. The rabbi registered and trademarked the word "SpeedDating" as a single word. This left the two words, "speed dating," free for the rest of the world to use. The very first speed-dating gathering occurred in Beverly Hills in 1998. It didn't take long for the concept to become a commercial success, and it still is popular today throughout the United States.

If you have never participated in speed dating before, you'll be happy to hear that it really is quite fun! Men and women meet for a quick-paced evening of mini-dates that last from five to ten minutes each. After each mini-date, the leader either clinks a glass or rings a bell to signal time to move to the next dating station. At the end of the session, everybody gives the leader a list of selected desired dates. Of course, contact information is confidential. The rules do not allow any phone number sharing during the initial meeting. This way you don't have to reject a suitor in person. You also won't feel rejected should the tables be turned. If there is a match or matches, the leader will provide you with that list later. It's up to you and your potential dates to take it further.

Several such events are scheduled regularly across the United States and throughout the United Kingdom. Many occur through clubs and organizations, as well as religious affiliations. They often cater to a niche group, such as theatergoers or people who love to travel. Others are strictly for marriage-minded individuals. You will be pleased to know that one of the most popular speed-dating parties is geared toward women and younger guys. Just last night I watched a TV special featuring a popular nightclub in Florida that regularly hosts Boy Toy speed dating for women and younger men.

What to Ask

Since speed dating is so fast, many women worry about what kinds of questions they should ask the guys. The first word of advice I give my clients when they question me on what to ask is, if you have to ask, don't ask! Let me simplify. If you are not sure about whether something is appropriate, it is best not to ask. The first few seconds are always the toughest. Start with a smile. Be prepared ahead of time with a series of questions that make you feel comfortable. This is not a job interview, but you still want to appear at your best. Remember—always be true to you. Following are a few good speed-dating questions:

- What are three words that best describe you?
- What do you do for fun?
- What color describes you, and why?
- If you could live anywhere, where would it be?

What Not to Ask

When meeting for such a short date it is best to avoid any heavy questions. That is, of course, unless he's a body-builder talking about his weight. Asking a Boy Toy what he does for a living is not very original at a speed-dating party. Avoid politics and anything about his mother. Whatever you do, don't start talking about any ex-boyfriends, ex-husbands, or his ex-girlfriends. Younger men are full of dreams and ambitions that they are eager to share. Younger women are too into themselves to listen to these guys. Perhaps the best strategy is not to ask any questions—let *him* talk! This is not about appearing submissive. You already know about you. This gives you the chance to pick the younger man of your choice. He can always listen to you later on your one-on-one dates. If he doesn't pick you, it's his loss!

Date Safely

Being a Boy Toy Babe can leave a girl feeling giddy, youthful, and filled with joy. That is truly part of what makes dating a younger man so much fun. However, I feel that, as an author, it would be irresponsible of me to neglect addressing the importance of dating safely. Just because a man is younger does not mean he is less likely to be an ax murderer or rapist. Whatever age your potential mate may be, I implore you to always date with safety in mind!

This advice is particularly important when dating Boy Toys. I'm not saying that Boy Toys are necessarily more dangerous than older men. Bad men come in all shapes, sizes, and ages. It's just that our common sense is more likely to tell us to be cautious with an older man. With a Boy Toy, it is easier to let your guard down. The nature of many women is to be nurturing. This can put you at great risk if you throw caution to the winds for even a fleeting moment. With a younger guy you can easily forget these words of wisdom, especially when the younger man may be the same age as your son. This can give you a false sense of safety.

Say you meet a new guy and your heart is aflutter. He's young, handsome, and dresses really well. You are totally charmed that a complete stranger appears to know the deepest part of your soul. He even appears sensitive, everything you have ever wanted in a man. Creating feelings like these is often how serial killers operate. How many women have unknowingly fallen prey to these sick members of our society? Many innocent women have succumbed to the seduction of these predators only to end up as victims. According to figures from the FBI, U.S. Department of Justice, a woman is raped every two minutes somewhere in America. Seventeen percent of these rapes are committed not by a stranger, ex-husband, or live-in boyfriend, but by an acquaintance—an acquaintance with whom the victim feels safe enough to be alone. When it comes to female homicide, women are substantially more likely than men to be murdered by someone they know. In fact, an assailant known to the victim commits one-third of all female homicides, and of those female victims, the greatest age range falls between 30 and 50. Don't become tomorrow's headlines and another statistic—date safely!

Dating Safety Advice

Going out on a first date with a complete stranger can be nerve-racking at any age. If your best friend has known the guy for years, you may feel a little more comfortable about your safety. However, when meeting a perfect stranger, I prefer to set up "chat-up" meetings rather than first dates. This is the time to exercise extreme caution! Meet him in a safe, well-lit area that has lots of people around. Coffee shops and bookstore cafés are perfect for this. Do not feel ill at ease about repeating several chat-up meetings before you have the actual first date—and even then, you must be cautious! Never meet him in some out-of-the-way place such as a hotel room. For goodness' sake, do not ride alone in his car or meet him at his residence or yours. Use your noggin!

Cyndi's Secrets™

When meeting a younger man who lives out of town, it is best to set up your "chat-up" sessions in your territory. For safety, he should stay in a hotel. However, should you have to travel to his area, give his contact information to everyone who cares about you. Let him know that everyone has his number. Many women ask their female friends or their adult children to hang out for the first meeting. It's not quite as romantic, but for a casual meet-and-greet it is perfectly acceptable. Enlist one of your platonic guy friends to show up accidentally on purpose. You can introduce the two. It's a great way to let the new Boy Toy know that someone is looking out for you. Just make sure it is truly a platonic friend so there is not an issue of male rivalry. You can also choose to double-date. Having your sister and her husband or a couple of friends share dinner can be fun and safe. You can get their feedback later.

Boy Toy Talk

"I was having a pastry dessert with a new Boy Toy dish. We were at a downtown French café. I asked my longtime best friend Harry to show up for safety reasons. My daughter Chloe, who is 25, usually swings by for these first-time meetings but she was on a date with her boyfriend. I thought it would be cool since Harry and I are friends. Okay—he's an "intimate" friend! You know—a friend with fringe benefits. Well, all I can say is, it is always better to be safe, but I was sorry I invited Harry. Opt for a purely platonic friend."

Sue, 50

Ask him where he works, and get references. You can call his business number or drop by. See how the receptionist responds when you mention his name. I find that it helps to be up-front about your concern for safety. Tell him that his contact information and your date with him are on your planner pad. Let him be aware that several people have his number and know about the date. Talk openly about how you must be careful these days with so many rapists and serial killers on the loose. Pay attention to how he responds. If he respects you, none of your questioning will bother him. Ask him to show you his driver's license. Do not show him yours. It's best not to let him know where you live until you feel sure about him. Take your time with as many chat-up sessions as you need to be safe. This may seem to take the fun out of dating, but it doesn't really. Think of it as just a part of life as we know it today. Being safe feels good and can help to increase your Boy Toy joy! You are worth the wait!

Meeting an Online Match

Earlier in this chapter, we talked about dating online. Internet dating comes with its own share of safety concerns. Since more and more women are meeting younger men on the Web, it's easy to start thinking it is safe. It is not! Please remember that if a Boy Toy can lie to you in person, he can easily lie to you on the Internet. Follow the same protective measures you would on any other date, and then some. Keep these safety tips in mind:

- Do not give out personal information. Avoid last names, phone numbers, or addresses. Do not mention where you work, schools attended, or names of family and friends.
- Use dating-site services for receiving messages rather than using your regular e-mail account. Most dating sites offer their own chatrooms and a personal e-mail address through their site as part of the service. There is no reason to give out your private e-mail address or any private information.
- Carry a cell phone with 911 programmed in. This is good to do for all first meetings, but particularly important when meeting someone off the Web.
- Follow your intuition. Never be afraid of offending your Web mate. It's better to be safe than sorry.

Predator Warning Signs

If only we had a clear picture of what a predator is supposed to look like, the world would be a much nicer place. But, we don't. In fact, many predators appear to be the "nicest" people. However, there are a few characteristics that many of them have in common. Obviously, there are normal people who exhibit some of these traits. That does not necessarily make them deviants. Use the following information as a guideline to help you size up a potential mate and protect yourself from predators:

- The goal of a sexual predator is to get you alone and isolated.
- A predator usually has a plan prepared. Watch him for any verbal or nonverbal cues.
- They often use alcohol for manipulation.
- Is he angry and abusive to cashiers and waiters?
- Does he grab you without your permission?
- Remember that he could be a Dr. Jekyll and Mr. Hyde. Take your time getting to know him.
- Does he criticize you excessively?
- Does he avoid eye contact?
- Survivors talk of not trusting their instincts. I've said this before—follow your gut! Listen to that little voice inside. It knows a lot. Trust it!
- Do not let him make you go someplace you don't want to go.
- Is he vague? Does he change his story or seem ambiguous?

Look—I'm not trying to be a killjoy here. Remember, you just met this man. Once you are safe and you like the guy you can follow up with some hot, romantic, fun, and even fulfilling stuff. Okay, steamy too! Let the Boy Toy Program continue!

Chapter 9

The First Date (or the Last)

······································
It's Okay—Have Fun!
······································

One Friday night my girlfriend Helena and I were at a hoity-toity Hollywood nightclub. We sat in the VIP area with a group of old farts. You know the type. They were trying to impress us with their cash, free-flowing champagne, and caviar. This area was forbidden fruit to many of the younger men, who did not make the cut. On the other side of the velvet ropes was a swarm of Boy Toys trying to peer in. Two of them caught our attention with their charming yet almost shy flirtatious ways. It did not take long for Helena and me to step outside the fortress. These two were brothers in their early 20s, and we delighted in their nervous energy as they chatted us up. Before the night ended, they invited us for a double date on that Saturday night. We accepted. You could see their enthusiasm swell as their chests puffed up with pride.

Helena and I did not take this all that seriously, and I doubt that the "boys" were thinking marriage. It just sounded like a fun evening. Perhaps a little ego boost for all four of us. Helena is a tall, exotic Greek beauty. I'm a petite Polish blonde. We dressed to the nines in little

97

sexy strapless cocktail dresses. To stay safe, we both drove together to meet our Boy Toys. We were set to go with stun guns, pepper spray, my kickboxing techniques, and her black belt in karate. We felt like a dynamite duo, but prepared.

Once arriving at their modest apartment building, we took the elevator to the third floor. In front of the door to their apartment, Helena and I did what hot Boy Toy Babes do before making an entrance. We fluffed our hair, lifted our puppies to enhance their magnificence, and got into one of those "I'm sexy but not a slut" poses. She knocked. He answered. We thought—"What!?" This was not a Boy Toy. He was a cute little white-haired 80-something-year-old Yiddish man! The three of us stared at each other open-mouthed for a moment. We were at the wrong apartment!

Meanwhile, the boys had begun drinking before we arrived because they were so nervous. When we finally got to the right apartment, they tried to act as if they were more mature while struggling with their drunken, slurred speech. Helena and I began to wonder what the heck we were doing there. After all, we were sophisticated women. Then the telephone rang. The 24-year-old picked up the phone and almost immediately, the 22-year-old passed out. It was their dad. Helena and I left. Needless to say, that was the last date with those boys.

Helena and I love to tell this story. We've laughed about it numerous times. It did not go the way we planned, but then what in life really does? She and I both have participated in fun, fearless female nights. I'm not even talking about sex, but just a fun evening in the company of a charming, adoring, and interesting young man. She and I each have also had relationships with younger men that were deep, intimate, and meaningful. The message I share from my experience, my friends' experiences, and from the numerous people who took my cybersurvey and interviews is that it is okay to desire the company of Boy Toys. You have choices. Boy Toys can increase your options as well as provide more opportunities for the happiness that you deserve. Whether you accept casual dates for friendship, lust for a young hardbody, or yearn for a long-term partnership based on love, give yourself permission to accept Boy Toys into your life. Do not deny yourself the pleasure of a Boy Toy date. I repeat—it's okay!

Avoiding Disasters

If you have decided that dating a younger man is for you, let me help you get through the dating process. Throughout this chapter, I will give you some great tips—everything from what to wear on your date with a young dude to what to say. I'll help you to avoid disasters before they happen.

What to Wear

Everybody tries to look his or her best on a first date. It's expected. If either person doesn't, it says, "I don't care enough about you to clean up." Even if you met a Boy Toy at the post office while you were in a sweatshirt and jeans, he expects to see you looking hot for your date. In fact, he is probably thinking about you constantly before the date occurs. Showing up to go out looking your "dating" best gives him two looks to compare. It will turn him on to think, "Wow! She looks great with or without makeup."

I love to take my time getting all done up for a date. No matter how much time you spend, you want to make it look like you didn't try "too" hard. The irony is that creating an effortless look is what often takes the most amount of time. Guys hardly ever understand our beauty rituals, but they love the results. Aim for the "WOW!" reaction. You can do it.

You might wonder whether to try to dress "younger" when going out with a Boy Toy. My response is that a hot Boy Toy Babe is ageless! Never ever, forget that pearl of wisdom. Do not dress to accommodate a number. Rather, dress to suit your personal style and body type. Use the following information to create your own unique look—at your "dating" best! Of course, there is nothing wrong with wanting to please your Boy Toy, but always remember that the most important element is to be true to you.

FINDING YOUR PERSONAL STYLE

My biggest fashion secret revolves around one basic philosophy about what I choose to wear. It goes like this: "I don't follow fashion; I make my own style!" My celebrity clients enjoy incorporating this philosophy into their wardrobe choices because it helps them to confirm their image. Each of us has a unique image. Call it your packaging. You need to present your best packaging to succeed at your Boy Toy date. Once you find your personal style, the fashion industry cannot control you. You're a Boy Toy Babe—nobody controls you. Discover how to strut your stuff on your personal catwalk. There's something very sexy about a woman with style.

To help you find your individual style, I've divided your potential dating wardrobe options into four categories. They are:

- Classic Chic
- Nature Girl
- High-Fashion Drama Queen
- Feminine Feline

You don't have to fit into one of these categories exclusively. Use My Style Sheet, which follows, to pinpoint your personal style. Discover the positive points that make your style unique in the Wardrobe Description. Use that information to build your wardrobe. There is also a column for a Fashion Alert! Each category has the potential for a fashion disaster. Being aware of potential mistakes can help you avoid them.

Cyndi's Secrets™

Almost 99 percent of the younger men I interviewed expressed a desire for women with a "feminine" look. They find that today's younger women are often too casual and "manly." Some experts may feel that this doesn't gel with the feminist movement. I disagree. I think women are equal but different. What could be more empowering than embracing our femininity? This doesn't mean you have to be ultra girlie if that is not your personality, but a soft touch here and there goes a long way to catch a man's eye.

MY STYLE SHEET

Personal Style	Wardrobe Description	Fashion Alert!
Classic Chic	Tailored, refined, elegant	Borderline boring
Nature Girl	Casual, easygoing	Too understated, sloppy
High-Fashion Drama Queen	Trendy, get noticed	Intimidating, too much drama
Feminine Feline	Romantic and feminine	Too little-girlish

Remember that this table is a guideline. Use it to bring out your own personality. Nobody says you can't be a combination of these styles, or change according to what is going on in your life, your moods, and of course your date. I enjoy playing with style. On one date I'll wear a Classic Chic suit paired with a Feminine Feline peekaboo cami top for a romantic touch. On another date, you can catch me in a trendy High-Fashion Drama Queen mini paired with rock-star boots and fishnets. The bottom line is that it is ladies' choice. Use My Style Sheet to help you represent that choice. To win a younger man's heart, let your outside package be representative of the inner you!

Cyndi's Secrets™

Talk to your Boy Toy ahead of time to discuss the dress code for your date. Be prepared to give a little direction in this department. Torn jeans and a backward baseball cap may be a younger man's norm, so he most likely will appreciate the coaching. For example, you might say, "Let's do casual chic tonight. I love it when a man dresses up, even if it's khakis and a shirt." Of course, many young men these days are style mavens. If so—get his advice.

Many dating experts suggest never wearing anything sexy on a first date. I say, "Grow up!" It's one thing to give this advice to a young teenage girl as she discovers who she is and begins to understand her body. However, you are a grown woman who knows her body and how to use it. I recommend dressing with lots of class and a dash of sex appeal. It could be as simple as a basic black dress cinched at the waist with a skinny red belt. It's about being totally "you" with a touch of something that lets him know he is special and you are interested.

ENHANCING YOUR BODY TYPE

Once you have determined your personal style, you need to take an honest look at your body type. Being honest about your body type can help you choose clothes that will make you look your best. This way you can look hot on your date with a Boy Toy and feel fabulous about yourself every day of your life! There are several different ways to study body types. For purposes of this program, I have divided body types into four categories:

1. **Hourglass:** This is a very curvy figure. Lucky girl—you have great *vavoom* potential. Avoid clothing that is too loose, which can make you look heavier. Opt for a tailored fit. On your first date, a pencil skirt can look hot on you. Dark colors and solids can be slimming. If you are in good physical shape, pastel colors can work perfectly. Avoid any garment gathered at the waist. This can create too much of a bulge.

2. **Pear:** Your lower body is bigger than the top. You look fabulous in suits and jackets that have slightly padded shoulders to balance your shape. I'm not talking the football pads of the 1980s. Avoid wearing bright bottoms with dark tops. Be Boy Toy ready and look perfectly smashing in a bright blousy look on the top with a dark bottom to give the illusion of a balanced body.

3. **Inverted Triangle:** Your upper body is bigger than your bottom. Boy Toys are in awe of your magnificent shoulders. You certainly do not need shoulder pads, so be sure to remove any from your current wardrobe. Look for clothes with vertical lines to give the illusion of a long, tall, and lean look. You can make an entrance on your first date in bright-colored pants and skirts paired with medium- to dark-toned tops.

4. **Apple:** You carry weight in the middle area. You look delicious in longer tops and jackets paired with skinny pants or pencil skirts. Avoid anything baggy, which can be blimpy. When you hang out with your favorite Boy Toy, wear horizontal lines on the top with a solid-color bottom. This takes the focus off your tummy so he can completely get into you!

First-Date Tips

Following are a few basic dating tips to help you through the Boy Toy Program. These are great whether you've been dating for eons or haven't dated in a long time. Getting back in the saddle is tough if you just got over a divorce, death of a partner, or you left the convent. Enjoy my first-date tips:

- **Be on time.** Okay, this is not one of my best characteristics, but it truly is important. If you tend to run late, as I often do, be sure to let your Boy Toy know that up-front. This way he knows to tell you that he will pick you up fifteen minutes before he actually plans on picking you up. This is the considerate thing to do so you both can respect each other's time frame. I also inform my date not to arrive a minute early. Heaven forbid I haven't removed the last Velcro roller before he sees me.
- **Be spontaneous.** Things often do not go as planned. Restaurants suddenly close, weather rains out events, and any number of unexpected things can occur. Roll with the punches. It often helps to have a backup plan.
- **Leave him wanting more.** Make it a short date. This serves a few purposes. First, it makes him crazy

with excitement about seeing you again. This is cool if you do like him. It also means that if he is less than the dream dude you had hoped for, you haven't invested too much time.

- **Flatterywill get you everywhere.** Everybody likes a compliment, and your Boy Toy is no exception. However, make sure it is sincere. Nothing makes people want to barf more than fake flattery. And never tie a compliment to a manipulative motive. A hot BTB should not partake of this unflattering nonsense.

- **Don't be a Chatty Cathy.** In the old days there was a popular doll named Chatty Cathy. Your Boy Toy probably never heard of her. Whether or not you have heard of the doll, the name says it all. Make sure you balance your conversation with talking and listening. Okay, you can yak a bit more than you would with an older man. Younger guys are usually better at listening, but be reasonable.

Chatting Him Up

Conversing with a younger man comes with its share of challenges. Don't freak out! Chatting gives each of you the chance to discover what is creating your connection. Is the attraction purely physical? Do you have anything else in common? Through asking questions and listening well you can discover the truth about your relationship. Once each of you is honest about what is drawing you together, you can both decide as mature adults whether you want to proceed, and how. Following are a few good tips for keeping the conversation flowing smoothly.

Generational Differences

Be prepared for generational differences. There will be things that are bound to come up, such as music preferences, pop culture figures, and slang terms, that may make you feel as if you are going into unknown territory. Rather than feel old about the age gap, view it as an adventure well worth exploring. Many young men may enjoy hearing what you have to say. Remember, these guys listen! They also feel a sense of pride as manly men who can teach you the ways of "their" world.

What Does He Like to Do Outside of Work?

This is an excellent question to ask a younger man. Even if he has a decent job at the bank and seems mature, his off time says a lot about him. If the conversation suddenly switches to his life of video games 24/7 with his buds, you may think differently about moving forward with him—that is, unless video games are something that interests you too. A hot BTB always makes her own choices!

The Fear Factor

If the fear factor strikes, relax. The fear factor occurs when you are on a date with a younger man and suddenly feel you don't belong. Several things can cause this feeling. It may come about after witnessing giggling girls at the next table, or catching an innocent glance at your own reflection on the dinner plate. Snap out of it! It's the image in the plate that is distorted, not you. When this feeling occurs, take a deep breath and give him the "look." You know, the one where you tilt your head downward and look up with your eyes. This gives you a chance to pull yourself together while he gets lost in your eyes. Besides, you can factor in the fear factor for him, too. Trust me—he's more nervous than you are!

It Is What It Is

Make sure you really listen to what he says. For example, if he tells you he doesn't want children for another fifteen years, or perhaps none at all, he probably really means that. This is important, because if your biological clock is about to go *boom*, you may think twice before proceeding with this stud. Younger men often give pertinent information about themselves in the early stages of dating. Women do not always listen. Perhaps this is because you are so used to being around older men who do not express themselves. Take advantage of any tidbit of information you can.

Topics to Avoid

Whether he is younger or not, first-date impressions are lasting. Many experts say it's important to avoid controversy at the beginning of a relationship, so don't head straight into the topic of politics unless it's an absolute deal-breaker for you. However, the cool thing about dating a younger man is that it's really quite acceptable to show him a bit of your spirit—even on a first date. Feel free to express your opinion about topics that make you passionate. This is where a younger man can outshine the older ones. He will more than likely see your thoughts as strength, whereas an older man may think of you as domineering or overbearing. A critical component is essential for this formula to work. You must balance your powerful position with your *softer* side. Pay attention! Conversation needs an ebb and flow to tantalize. It is very appealing to show that you are a woman of strength, but never pretend that you aren't vulnerable. In fact, isn't that combination what we women constantly claim we want from our men? Think about it!

Usually when I give dating advice, I recommend finding out how your man feels about his mother. This can shed some light as to whether he respects women. This, however, is not the case when having a first date with a Boy Toy. Talk about his mom and you run the risk of appearing as if you hang out with her pack. Yikes! This can ruin a sexy and romantic evening. The last thing you want to do is unknowingly give the impression that you are a "mommy" to him. Granted, there are some successful relationships in which the woman enjoys being a parental figure to a Boy Toy. If that's you—go for it. You know that I believe in being honest with your partner and yourself, and in welcoming choice. However, most BTBs prefer to avoid an over-nurturing role. Many of you already have children and long to feel free. You can always find out later how he feels about his mom, and discover whether he respects women. Don't scare him off with maternal matters on the first date.

Leave Your Baggage at Home

Many younger men in my survey were very open about what made their relationships work—or not. I was amazed at how often a woman's emotional baggage destroyed the prospect of a loving future partnership. Perhaps there is a lesson here for us all. In the way that women detest older men who hang on to old issues, we should let go too. Do not become jaded. To go forward with a young Boy Toy you must release the part of your past that is dragging you down, especially on a first date!

Say you and a Boy Toy meet for coffee and your cute roommate happens to walk by. Your BT might innocently say, "She seems nice." This could trigger the memory of your cheating ex, who thought lots of women were "nice." Going off on a tangent about how all men cheat and lie is not fair to him or his gender and could drive him away. You might think this is casual conversation, while he views it as anger. What you think is opening up about your life may be closing the door to a new relationship.

This baggage may be a desperate plea for pity or even an outright need to be confrontational. Neither is attractive to a Boy Toy. Digging deeper, anger is a secondary emotion. The first is feeling hurt. If you don't deal with your hurt in a healthy manner, it'll keep resurfacing as anger out of nowhere. Don't bite every potential mate with these displaced feelings. Take time to deal with your emotional baggage before it morphs into anger. Work through your issues—we've all got them. Seek counseling if you need to.

Boy Toy Talk

"I dated Sue, who was 35. It lasted for a year. It was good while we were together. The sex was great and I consider her a lifetime friend. However, when she gets upset there is too much drama. Too many guys have messed with her head and I was the one who had to deal with it. I wanted to enjoy life and her companionship. The age difference backfired on me and I ended up being the teacher."

Casey, 28

"We met recently a second time after both of our spouses died. It was a short affair through the autumn. We kept each other amused. We never bored each other, as our collective egos would not allow it. It's too bad that we hadn't met earlier because we could've been a team, like Burns and Allen. I tried to help her, but she could not let go of her past."

Garth, 53

Ending a Date: Kiss or Kiss-Off!

Dates can be wonderful, horrible, or just so-so. However, they all eventually end. Whether your date concludes with a kiss or a kiss-off is part of what makes the process interesting, fun, and sometimes irritating. Following are some tips for ending your date:

- If a date did not go well but he was a nice guy, be honest with your Boy Toy. I don't mean saying something mean; just make it clear that you are not interested. There is nothing wrong with telling your date that you appreciate him but that you don't see this working out. Ask him not to take it personally. It's even kind to say that you just want some time to yourself. Chances are that he doesn't feel the connection either and will be relieved that you said it first.
- Even good dates need to end. Be prepared to graciously exit before he does. Being a step ahead in this department gives you a mysterious edge that feeds into his hunter's instinct.
- If the dude you date is a dud, ditch the good-night kiss. Let's face it—if you give him any physical attention, a younger man is going to misread the signals. Save yourself the headache and take care of this matter pronto!
- When the date is winding down and you are with someone you really like, it is very alluring to share how much you have enjoyed yourself. This sets the stage for reciprocation. Should he respond positively—bingo! If you don't get his feedback, he is either not interested, a game player, or perhaps too shy. In any case, remember that you are a hot BTB. Therefore, proceed with confidence!

- He's young, a hunk, and all over you in the physical department. Perhaps you are not ready to move as quickly as he is. This does not mean he is a bad person, as long as he respects your boundaries. If you are prepared to physically move faster than he is, be respectful of his feelings too. If you are both fired up—well, you're all grown up, so making the decision to wait or not is your choice! Just exercise caution and be certain the two of you are on the same page.
- Ending the date without any physical contact such as a kiss or hug does not mean you are doomed. It actually can be quite charming. Younger men know you come with experience, and many fancy taking their time. Some want to show you that they respect you, which is sweet and nice. Others are just plain nervous. Enjoy the simplicity of this innocent phase. Who knows where this journey may take you!

Chapter 10

The Woos and Woes of Dating

Let Him Chase You

There is an old saying that goes like this: "He chased her till she caught him." That statement still rings true today. Men of all ages love a good chase. Does this mean you have to resort to game playing? Not at all. It just means you don't have to pounce on him like a cougar predator going after her prey to get what she wants. It's wooing season—enjoy it! If the wooing ends, you don't want woes to begin. Later in the program, I'll show you how the wooing doesn't have to stop should you move forward into a lasting relationship.

For now, let's dabble in our wooing dating desires. Many young men are superb at wooing, since they really are determined to show you that they can please you. It's nice to see the kind of effort a younger man can make when you compare him to old codgers. Past bad relationships have jaded so many of those older guys.

Wooing by a younger man may be slightly different from that of the older men you have known. Younger men usually get very nervous when dating an experienced woman. They often fear that they aren't up to your standards. Boy Toys need extra coaxing or reassurance that you are open to their advances. Be sure to give them a big sign that you are interested. Many times, one signal isn't enough for the Boy Toy. Even if it is the third date and the two of you are hitting it off, make sure you continue to let him know you are interested. For example, when the date ends you can say something that gives him a suggestion for the future. If you just returned from a fun afternoon of playing golf you might say, "Nice round of golf, let's do it again." This gives him the opportunity to woo you with confidence. If his response is, "Yes, that was fun, I really enjoyed it," you know the relationship is proceeding on par.

Boy Toy Talk

"I was a 26-year-old student going to college when I met Reina. She was definitely all 'woman.' Reina worked in student affairs. She was a fair-skinned Persian beauty with long black hair. I loved that she was voluptuous! In my country of Srilanka we would say "chunky," but that word doesn't go over well here in the States. I had seen her in the office a few times on school business. Boy was I attracted to her. However, I couldn't approach this goddess. I feared she might think I was just a kid. One day I went in for some help and she blurted out that it was her 31st birthday. I jumped at the chance to find out the scoop on her story, so I immediately inquired about the fun plans I assumed she would be having. "I have no plans," she reported. I acted shocked and after she repeated her lack of plans three times, I finally got the hint! Yesss! Thank God, she gave me a sign. I took her out for sushi and a movie. She was totally impressed that I was romantic enough to ask her out in front of her coworkers. We had a wonderful time for two months. She wanted a committed relationship and I was not ready. Eventually we went separate ways. When I think of radiant Reina I look back and smile."

Rohan, 26

Of course, you can woo too. Countless little acts of kindness show a Boy Toy your affection. I'm not referring to spending tons of money on lavish gifts. I'm talking about paying attention to him and responding. For example, if you know that he is collecting research for a work project on saving the planet, you can give him some statistics you found while doing a Google search. If the planet is his passion and you agree, volunteer to start recycling.

Always show appreciation for any gifts he may give you. Men have always enjoyed adorning women, throughout the ages. Do not deny him this pleasure. Quite honestly, most of us like the ritual. If you make more money than he does, do not let that affect your appreciation of his thoughtfulness.

Letting him catch you may be great wooing fun, but it comes with a wooing warning. Take heed! There are times in nature where the less you want him, the more he wants you—or the less he wants you, the more you want him. We all, at times, want what we can't have. When this starts to happen, you need to step back and evaluate why you are pursuing this relationship. Is it about winning at the conquest, or is it wooing in its purest form? To win at the wooing game you need to discover whether your relationship is happening for the right reason.

The Courtship

Wooing sometimes seems to have become a lost art. You hear about couples who have one-night stands. Others glue themselves together at the hip after the second or third date. Whatever happened to good old-fashioned courtship? You know—when a guy takes a girl out and they take their time getting to know each other. Each person is up-front that there is not a commitment since the relationship is too new. This ups the stakes a little higher, but it can make the courtship even more fun.

I have a theory that you can ruin a relationship by expecting too much too soon. That's how you set yourself up for failure. Nowadays, couples go on a date and if they have a nice time, each starts to assume that the other one is not seeing anyone else. Why can't we all just be honest up-front and allow for a "getting to know you" time frame? I'm not talking five years of "I'm not committed to you, but let's have sex." I'm talking about a fair amount of time to discover whether this is someone you truly want to try to go solo with. There seems to be an important middle dating stage that is missing in our culture.

Let me explain further. Nowadays, a guy asks a girl out. If she accepts, he practically assumes that she is his girlfriend. The "You are my property" syndrome kicks in. A woman, on the other hand, often avoids going on dates if she doesn't feel instant euphoria toward a man. She is afraid of trying to shake his "claim" on her before the claim is ever made. No wonder there are a lot of lonely people walking this earth. I believe that both men and women want so badly for relationships to work that we expect too much too soon. We immediately project what we want our partners to be before we know who they really are. Who among us can live up to that fantasy? As an expert dater, let me tell you, this cannot work.

How does this apply to our dear Boy Toys? They too have been raised to instantly "claim" a woman. This comes from ages of social conditioning. The good news is that younger men are not as set in their ways as the older men. Remember, they listen to you. This leaves you in a remarkable position to break this age-old pattern. How, you ask? Be honest about wanting to discover everything about each other.

Allow a courtship to take place. A loving, warm, and wonderful courtship with a younger man is something that is easily within your grasp. Go ahead and date, laugh, explore, and have fun! See other people if you desire, while he can see others too. Be prepared to accept the risk of losing him. Trust that this discovery period can help you avoid problems later. Only until the two of you have spent some quality time together should you even broach the topic of exclusivity. Enjoy the wooing!

Picking Up the Tab: Who Pays?

When it comes to dating, many hot BTBs are in a quandary over who picks up the tab. Do not fret about this. Even experts can't come to terms on this matter. It seems that everybody has a different take. On one hand, there is pressure for a woman to contribute the larger share if she makes more money than the man does. This philosophy is screaming out to women dating younger men because they usually make more money than do their Boy Toys. The strong feminist backlash says, "Fine—if you can burn your bra, you can burn a hole in your wallet at the same time!" Of course, not all sentiments are that severe. Some feel that if a woman is equal and liberated, she should pay half of everything. They call this way of dating "Dutch treat." Each party pays his or her share. The extreme other end of the camp says the man should pay for everything. Chivalry is alive and well for these traditional thinkers. Certainly, there are options in between; maybe you take turns paying, or one pays most of the time. With all this confusion, one thing is for sure: determining who pays is much more than a "who's loaded" question.

If you subscribe to the notion that whoever makes the most money should pay, you are setting yourself up for disaster. I realize that there is a good chance that you make more money than a younger man does. Let me remind you that we are discussing the early dating stage. There should be lots of wooing going on. It's hard enough for a younger man to feel like a "man" when he knows you are so experienced. If you don't *allow* him to pay most of the time, he may come to resent you.

Cyndi's Secrets™

Never feel that just because a Boy Toy buys you dinner that you have to give him sex. Intimacy must always be a mutual choice between two people. Be prepared for some young men who will see you as an easy lay. This old stereotype still exists these days. Remind yourself that it is his privilege to take you to dinner.

In the past, when asked who should pay, I would squirm. This troubled me because frankly, I hardly ever pay during the initial dating stage, no matter what age the man or his income. Okay—I'll be even more up-front: I like it that way. My personal life is separate from my professional life. Maybe there is a little bit of an old-fashioned girl underneath it all. Who would have thought? This does not mean that I act like a prima donna and never contribute—of course not! I love to pop for the popcorn or spring for a chicken dinner on occasion. It's important to be giving, gracious, and appreciative of each other. Everybody likes to feel that each person in the potential partnership is thoughtful. So, pay for the parking if it makes you feel better.

Keep in mind that our focus here is on the early stages of dating, where the man is wooing *you!* He's wooing you even if you are the one more interested. Don't worry, I'll explain all that further in the Boy Toy Program. I realize that you may be used to finer restaurants and a fancier lifestyle than your Boy Toy can afford. If you like him enough and he likes you in return, you'll find plenty of less expensive restaurants, things to do, and places to see.

Now, that being said—I consider myself a modern woman and try to stay open to new thoughts and ways of doing things. Therefore, I realize that many of you are still going to want to pay. Okay, you are a big girl and the choice is yours. However, the real message I deliver is that you should never become the sole provider of dating funds. Share, split, take turns, let him pay, but do not become the meal ticket. Some experts say that whoever does the asking should also pay. Be sure you are not the only one doing the asking. Are you still confused? Here is my best advice: Go out and have a great time! Let the relationship take its course. Each situation is different. Always remember—you are a hot Boy Toy Babe and deserve to be treated as such!

BTB Cost Analysis

In light of all the fuss about women contributing financially throughout the courtship, I want to throw out a few thoughts for you to consider. Many women feel guilty if they don't share 50/50 in the early-stage dating funds. They think if we want equal pay, we'd better pay for our dates. Yet we still make almost one-quarter less than a man. That means even if your Boy Toy currently makes less than you, he may catch up soon!

Nobody mentions other factors, either. Are you aware that it usually costs twice as much for a woman to get ready for a date? It's so much more expensive being a woman— especially the kind of woman the Boy Toys in my cybersurvey and interviews tell me they want. She should take good care of herself. They want a woman who is feminine, sexy, smart, and dresses hot. Many want you to pull out all the bells and whistles so that they can whistle. Ladies, you know that looking hot does not come cheap!

Think about these variables. Our silk stockings alone can cost $20. Usually, the first time you wear them they get a run. He pays $5 for a pair of socks and you can't get him to throw them away. According to many dry cleaners, it costs a woman 10 to 15 percent more to maintain her wardrobe than it does for a man. His haircut is, on average, $15. Yours—$35, and that's a conservative estimate. Let's face it: most of us do some kind of color or streaking, which can up the cost close to $200. A simple white bra from a leading lingerie store can cost $31.50, and that's on "sale." Plain white granny panties can run $12. Of course, the price goes up when you add some pretty lace, satin, or silk. Buy a sexy G-string and find out quickly that less is *more!* He spends $25 for a year's supply of men's briefs. We buy lipstick, other makeup, creams, and have acrylics painted on our fingers. Don't even get me talking about the cost of shoes. Sure, men wear nice clothes. However, we show up in different outfits more frequently. This is not to sound as if I am complaining. I would be the first to admit I relish all the rituals of being a woman. I also say bravo to the hot BTBs who manage to stay beautiful and earthy at a lower cost. Revel in your own uniqueness. Of course, there are also men who are into excessive grooming and spend quite a bit too. However, by and large, this is not the case. Perhaps that is why there are no real clear-cut answers when it comes to who pays. Do what feels right for you! However, never, under any circumstances, feel pressured into covering all costs.

Boy Toy Talk

"When I was 10 I baby-sat Jake. A year ago we reconnected. At first, we would hang out together. Eventually we became really good friends. He's 26 and I'm 35, so I never knew my feelings could be so strong with such an age difference. However, now I want to take the relationship to a new level. We always take turns paying when we go out but it makes me feel like we are still 'just friends.' I long for a 'date' with him. I want to feel special."

Shaniqua, 35

Do NOT Be a Sugar Mommy

There are women who feel compelled to be sugar mommies. They fall into two distinct types. The first type of sugar mommy is the female counterpart to a sugar daddy. She lavishes her Boy Toy with gifts, trips, and anything he wants or desires. Many even pay the living expenses of these young hunks, making them "kept" men. The sugar mommy gets her reward with sex from her young virile stud whenever she desires. He is always available at her beck and call. This cougar predator type keeps her young prey caged under the guise of caring for them. If you look deeper, you discover it is usually more about control and power. The sugar mommy has a false sense of ownership. She is convinced that her Boy Toy will never leave her. Unfortunately, he usually does. These relationships very rarely last. If they do, you can bet the Boy Toy most often develops a strong sense of hate and resentment.

The second type of sugar mommy is truly motherly and can be overly attentive. Perhaps you are in a financially secure position and have a tremendous nurturing quality. You may have spent your whole life taking care of your ex-husbands, your children, and aging parents. For you, being a sugar mommy may not be about control, but about being a caretaker. You may actually love this younger man and want to do everything you can for him. Please hear me out. It is not your responsibility to take care of your Boy Toy. Doing so may emasculate him. This is particularly useful information when you begin a new relationship that has you head over heels. Take a step back and realize that you can shape the direction in which this new chapter in your life is taking you. Maybe it's time for someone to care about you, too! Find a way to help him help himself. Enjoy the pleasure of making him happy, but within reasonable limits. Counter your need to nurture by discovering how to receive gifts from him. Be gracious when he gives you a gift or does something nice. Even if he is poor and the gift isn't that great, let him know it truly is the thought that counts.

Boy Toy Talk

"After getting over my very young and foolish 'feministic' independence . . . I NEVER pay, no matter what age the man. After all, they have the honor of being in my company!"

Diana, 52

Real-Life Canoodling Capers

I thought it would be fun and helpful to include some real-life "canoodling capers" from my research. "Canoodling" is the term Hollywood uses to describe the wooing period of dating. It usually coincides with snuggling in public. Use these examples to help give you the courage to start dating the younger man. Whether your dates end up as a woo or a whoa, they usually are worth the effort. Besides, it takes lots of canoodling capers if you choose to go for a permanent partner. This first example comes from a Boy Toy who dated a hot BTB. She did not end up being his soul mate. However, he feels his life is better because of their connection and the time he spent wooing her. Even if you go into a relationship with a younger man that does not work out, you just might end up feeling more enriched:

"Lisa was 33 when we met, and I was 21. We were a couple for ten months. It was fun, eventful, and I loved learning about different things that my friends were not into at the time. It was scary at first, but we related well and really enjoyed each other's company. It was a great growing experience for me (outside of the bedroom as well). I learned a lot about myself as well as what I wanted down the line."

Jake, 33

Boy Toy Talk

"At 32, I fell in love with a man who was only 28. I realize now that it wasn't such a big age difference but back then, it bothered me. I was used to dating much older and very rich men who wined, dined, and bought me presents. Ron didn't make much money, but he was totally adoring and kind and we always had fun. I remember we were celebrating Christmas at his apartment. I never expected it, but he bought me a diamond pendant. It wasn't the biggest stone I ever got. However, till this day, I never got one that was more meaningful. He worked so hard saving his money. I know it was a sacrifice. Yet he was so happy to give it to me. It was out of love! I know that now. Sometimes I wish I hadn't left this man. He loved me and I didn't see it."

Patty, 68

In some of my research, pure sex and life experience were the common denominators. Truthfully, these relationships do not usually last. Here are a few of those stories.

"He was 24. We regarded each other's life like someone would be curious about an alien. With his longer-than-shoulder-length hair and punk/goth/gender-bender wardrobe, he didn't fit into my world. With my white-collar corporate career path, we just weren't a long-term fit. We both knew it and enjoyed each other immensely while we could. He gave me a touch of a wild side; I gave him acceptance from a stuffy normal segment of the population."

Becky, 32

"I was 23 when I met Daphne, a 39-year-old flight attendant. She walked into the retail lingerie store where I worked. It was a year of personal growth and sexual bliss. She taught me a lot. Everyone should try it once. Try it, you'll like it."

Carter, 47

Canoodling with a Boy Toy can do wonders for your ego. Enjoy the wooing while it is happening. However, do not use the experience as a validation of your self-worth. That is wooing gone wrong. Instead, focus on who you are as a beautiful person in your own right—ready to give and receive love.

"While in my 30s and 40s I dated guys in their 20s. Sex was fabulous! I think it came down to my ego, and just how darn flattering it was to be loved by someone so much younger (and so cute, too)! Plus I was able to show them a few things. I eventually stopped dating for a year to focus on me. . . . That is when I met my husband."

Rebecca, 53

Many spirited, hot BTBs reported strong opinions about the woos that occurred while canoodling with a Boy Toy. Their opinions, though varied, are all passionate and strong about the benefits of dating a younger man. This is just a sampling:

"I have dated men within ten years younger than I and it went very well. The best part about the relationship was their unending energy, both sexually and just joy for life in general."

Virginia, 52

"I have 'enjoyed' myself with at least fourteen young men (at last count). Usually they were just my 'boy toys.' There was one relationship that endured for 1½ years; he was 30, I was 40; and he wanted to marry me. There was also a young boy of 20 (I was 30) who wanted to marry me because he said he was so very bored sexually with his last girlfriend. He came from a family of wealth, so I knew he wasn't after my money since he had more than I had. It was sweet."

Diana, 52

Moving On

When the wooing stops, it is time to say whoa! You and your Boy Toy need to take a step back and evaluate the current state of affairs. If your Boy Toy is moving on, do not blame your age. You've invested enough time in the

Boy Toy Program to know that age is not an issue in most breakups with younger men.

What if you are the one who is tired of his midnight video game madness and want to move on? I implore you not to make the mistake of assuming all young men are off limits. One bad Boy Toy blunder does not warrant wiping out an entire generation of potential dates. A breakup just means you have to move on.

Cyndi's Secrets™

When a relationship with a Boy Toy falls apart, it is important not to blame a whole generation of younger men for the breakup. We are all individuals and should never be lumped into an age category stereotype. Do you like it when people stereotype you? Open your heart again to the option of men of all ages.

Here are a few tips to ease the pain of your Boy Toy dating woes:

- **Show a little class.** If the relationship didn't work, you should move forward with dignity. Even if the ending was nasty, resist any temptation to exact revenge. Hold your head up high, walk tall, and review the Controlled Crying segment of this program.
- **Avoid the things that remind you of him.** Take down the photos (it's okay to store rather than trash), throw out his toothbrush, and give him his belongings back.
- **Quit driving past his work and house.** This does nothing to help you heal. It reeks of stalker behavior. Did you forget that you are a hot BTB? It's time to move on.

- **Focus on enriching your life.** Have fun as an individual and with friends. More Boy Toys are always around the bend. Have faith that you can find a good one. Believe that being alone is cool, too. It's better than settling for less.
- **Resist the replacement.** When going through a breakup, it's very easy to reach for a quick replacement. Rebounds may work in basketball, but usually don't score high if you are thinking about a long-term relationship with a boy toy. If you can't keep yourself from going for the rebound, at least be up-front with the replacement about the play.

Date Him or Dump Him

Finding a younger man may be one thing, but whether you should date him or dump him is a completely different matter. Following is my Boy Toy Rating Scale. I created this as a lighthearted measurement of your mate's potential for you.

This is not a deep psychological or scientific test. Do not use it as a predictor of the ultimate fate of you and your Boy Toy. Take the test with a mind open to discovery, and maintain a spirit of fun. Use the results as a guideline for constructive talk between you and your Boy Toy. Be truthful. Enjoy!

Boy Toy Rating Scale

The following questions are multiple choices. Please select one of these answers for each of the questions.

A=ALWAYS, B=OFTEN, C=SOMETIMES, D=RARELY
E=NEVER

1. Do you and your Boy Toy laugh at the same jokes?
   a   b   c   d   e

2. Does your Boy Toy share his feelings with you when something is upsetting him?
   a   b   c   d   e

3. Does your Boy Toy speak about you with pride?
   a   b   c   d   e

4. Does your Boy Toy listen to you when you talk?
   a   b   c   d   e

5. Do you and your Boy Toy argue constructively?
   a   b   c   d   e

6. Do you and your Boy Toy have similar interests and enjoy each other's activities?
   a   b   c   d   e

7. Does your Boy Toy treat your age difference as a compliment to you (or is he at least discreet about it in front of his friends)?
   a   b   c   d   e

8. Does your Boy Toy support you in front of family and friends who do not approve of your age difference?
   a   b   c   d   e

9. Does your Boy Toy pay for a fair share of expenses?
   a   b   c   d   e

10. Will your Boy Toy pay for parking or valet so that you don't have to walk a mile while you are wearing stilettos? (In other words, he's not cheap!)
    a   b   c   d   e

11. Does your Boy Toy keep his anger in check?
    a   b   c   d   e

12. Does your Boy Toy make you feel content, comfortable, and safe?
    a   b   c   d   e

13. Do you and your Boy Toy exhibit physical attraction equally toward each other?
    a   b   c   d   e

14. Aside from the sexual attraction, does he make you feel that he really likes you?
    a   b   c   d   e

15. Does your Boy Toy make you feel happy?
    a   b   c   d   e

Now that you have completed the Boy Toy Rating Scale, you can add up your results. Give yourself five points for every "A," four points for every "B," three points for every "C," two points for every "D," and one point for every "E." Calculate your total points. Check out your results in the next segment to see where your Boy Toy weighs in.

Interpreting Your Results

Now comes the fun part! Check out the following chart to see where your man weighs in. Once you have determined how great he is, compare your score with the descriptions that follow.

Boy Toy Types	Total Points
Boy Toy Keeper	61 to 75 points
Boy Toy Friend	46 to 60 points
Boy Toy Stud	31 to 45 points
Boy Toy Dud	30 points or fewer

Now check to see what these ratings mean:

- **Boy Toy Keeper:** If your man weighs in as a Boy Toy Keeper, consider yourself lucky. He appears to be top choice. So far the two of you are communicating at all levels. You might consider dating him further to find out if he can continue to be a treasure. This one is a gem!
- **Boy Toy Friend:** A man weighing in as a Boy Toy Friend early in the relationship has the potential of climbing up the scale. You might want to give him a chance and continue to date him. After some time passes, take the quiz again. Many times a Boy Toy Friend can become a Keeper or remain the ultimate Boy Toy bud!
- **Boy Toy Stud:** The Boy Toy Stud can be a fun way to pass the time. However, is he really what you're looking for? Decide what you want out of life. If you need a notch in your bedpost, the Boy Toy Stud may be worth dating. However, if you are looking for a relationship that is lasting, don't waste your time on this dude!
- **Boy Toy Dud:** The Boy Toy Dud is not worthy of you. If he scores this low early in the relationship, how do you expect to change him? Dump him now lest you end up spending most of your life with a loser!

Hope you enjoyed this fun test. Of course, you need to know him on a deeper level for a long-term relationship to work. The character traits that you desire in a man are always your personal choice. However, this test information can help a hot BTB such as you determine whether to date him or dump him. Refer to it often until you find your ultimate Boy Toy!

Chapter 11

Sexy Secrets

The Art of Seduction

Oh, you are a little seductress! Did you skip to this part of the book because you saw the word "sexy" in the table of contents? Don't worry, that is very normal. Whether you've been following my Boy Toy Program from the start or are just peeking in now, let's dish about how you can use my sexy Cyndi's Secrets to win at the dating game. You can discover how to seduce him with your alluring charms.

Finding a Boy Toy is bound to make you feel sexy. Mastering the moves that let him know what you are thinking may be a little trickier. Must you be as blatant as Mrs. Robinson was in the movie *The Graduate*? It's far more scintillating to develop the *subtle* art of seduction. You can take the physical attraction between you and your Boy Toy to the point of intrigue, passion, and potentially love. Remember, you are a hot Boy Toy Babe! You move with grace, elegance, and a touch of class—never crass. If you throw yourself at a Boy Toy without the delicious sauce of seduction, you may miss many magnificent moments.

The art of seduction goes a step beyond friendly flirting. Friendly flirting is fun and shows a Boy Toy that you are interested. Seduction moves flirting forward, full speed ahead, with the intention of being sexually alluring to your younger man. It usually exhibits your desire for a mutual adult connection beyond platonic friendship. If you think about it, this whole book is about seduction. My Boy Toy Program prepares you to enjoy healthy, playful, and sometimes sultry seduction. Savor these tantalizing tips to seduce him.

Be Attentive

Give your Boy Toy 100 percent of your attention when you are with him. A younger man wants to feel he has all of you. His inexperience in life coupled with the pressure of being with a hot Boy Toy Babe can make him weak at the knees. It's only normal for him to be more insecure than an older man is. You can comfort him by figuring out what he genuinely wants you to notice. Is it his intelligence, accomplishments, looks, or all of the above? A good listener does more than say, "hmmmm," in between sentences. Focus on him and he will focus on you. If he doesn't focus back, lose your focus!

Use the Bend and Snap

This move became popular in the movie *Legally Blonde* when one of the characters, a manicurist, seduced the UPS man. She "accidentally on purpose" dropped an object so that she could bend over in front of him. She bent down from her waist to accentuate her butt, paused, and then snapped back up. The comedy exaggerated this move, of course, but when used discreetly it can work for you. Men never get tired of you showing off your body parts. You need to get his attention—though I'm teasing about making some big, bold, silly move. Subtlety is actually sexier. You can stroke your hair, slowly stretch your arms, or lengthen your waist. All of these are little moves that send him a big message. Even crossing your legs as you delicately scratch your ankle sends a signal.

To check whether a move is seductive, ask yourself, "Would I feel comfortable making this move in front of my best friend or sister?" If your answer is no, then you got it, baby!

Be Confident

Confidence is incredibly sexy. This does not mean you should act conceited about your many outstanding attributes. You know you are a hot BTB. Without your saying a word, he can tell that you are successful, talented, beautiful, and the picture of sophistication. Nobody on the stage, screen, or TV can come close to you. You are witty, charming, funny, and warm, and a siren compared to others. Why would he look any further? But remember, cockiness is not very appealing. Perhaps you are slightly insecure. Modest confidence is at the forefront of seduction.

Be Vulnerable

Balance your strength and the power of being a woman with vulnerability. This is not about being submissive, but showing that you also have a soft side. Being vulnerable is an incredibly seductive position. Start slowly in a new relationship. Be sure you are safe enough to let your guard down with this man. Your Boy Toy is younger but is just as capable of manipulation as an older man is. Opt for vulnerability via body language rather than through your heart early in the relationship. For example, appearing diminutive or coy for a brief moment is sexy and alluring without the risk of giving too much information. Eventually you can build to a point of showing vulnerability in all areas, including your heart. Build trust first.

Be Mysterious

When playing the seductress during early dating, it's best not to be too revealing. Physically and mentally, this is the time when it is appropriate to tease. Don't start out naked. Let everything about you unravel slowly. For example, if he asks you questions about yourself, choose to give short, sweet, and to-the-point answers. Don't have him pick you up at your home; that way he won't know where you live. This is safer and may make him crave you even more. This is not the time to give him the details of your deepest inse-curities or to brag about your villa in the mountains. Slowly peeling each other's layers can be very appealing.

Be Yourself

Tilting your head is coy and cute. This move can draw Boy Toys in like flies. It also can say, "I have a tic." Only use moves of seduction that are comfortable and work for you. Be true to you. Review the flirting tips in Chapter 7. Kick it up a notch!

Getting Naked

When the wooing is wonderful, it is bound to make you contemplate intimacy with your younger man. Don't be sur-prised if thinking about him makes your mouth water. Sure, you're a grown woman and the thought of getting naked is probably nothing new. However, there is something exhila-rating about the prospect of partaking of this young, virile stud. It's okay to feel this attraction. Rather than fight your sexual urges, why not explore them in a healthy manner. Begin by having a sex talk with your clothes on. If either you or your Boy Toy is not comfortable with this conversation, you should not be getting naked. These days it's a matter of life and death. Following is a "must discuss" list to include in your sex talk:

- **Sexual medical history:** Be sure to ask to see a recent AIDS test result. Talk openly and honestly about herpes and any other sexually transmitted diseases.
- **Condoms:** These are a "must" unless you are in a relationship that is 100 percent monogamous. First-time sex with a Boy Toy does not warrant condom-free sex.
- **Contraceptives:** What kind will be used, and who is providing it? This should be decided in advance.
- **Free to say no:** You or your Boy Toy may choose to hold off on having sex until you are married, engaged, or feel closer to each other. Having a sex talk while you're still clothed provides the opportunity to communicate where each of you stands. This allows for mutual respect.

When to Do the Deed

Nobody knows your body like you. It's okay to have fantastic feelings for a younger man! So the next question is, when is it okay to do the deed? Do not fall for some stupid rules such as, "Wait for the third date! Second is best! First is fine!" Give me a break! Whether he is 28 or 82, the time for intimacy is when you are ready for it. You hold the answer in your heart. Aim for the ultimate mind, body, and spirit connection. Oh—and of course, he must be ready too!

Remember to bear in mind that being intimate changes everything. There is no reason to rush into it. After nakedness, you will never see each other in quite the same way. This is not necessarily a bad thing. Make sure that you both are clear on whether you are dealing with lust, love, or both—or are you seeing the world through rosé-colored wineglasses?

Lights On or Off?

Getting naked for the first time in front of a new love can create anxiety for both men and women, regardless of age. With a younger man, your anxiety level may even be higher. It's particularly nerve-racking if you dwell on a few age spots or crow's feet. I implore you to see the beauty in a few soft lines and the skin-coloration changes of your life. Your Boy Toy knows you have lived, and that is often the attraction. Do not feel compelled to leave him in the dark unless you both sincerely like the lights out. Getting naked is supposed to leave both of you open to erotic exposure.

Boy Toy Talk

"I was having dinner with another date when Antonio spotted me. Secretly we exchanged numbers and this passionate, supportive, fun-loving man twelve years my junior swept me off my feet. We were together for four wonderful years. I remember I told Antonio I should wear my sunglasses all the time so people would not see my wrinkles. In the sunlight, he drew me in close to remove my glasses. With tender baby kisses, he caressed my crow's feet and told me how beautiful I was to him. I never felt so loved in my life. We broke apart because we ended up living in different towns and the distance was difficult. Age was never an issue—not with this man."

Katherine, 61

Now for a reality check. Having the lights on does not mean you have to have a spotlight shining on cellulite. There is nothing wrong with taking steps to help yourself feel and look like you are the hottest of the hot BTBs. Try these sexy tips to show yourself off in your best light:

- **Sheer silk scarf over a shade:** Everybody knows that candlelight is the most flattering. However, for a sensual twist, try covering your lampshade with a transparent silk scarf. I love to use a low-wattage soft pastel pink light bulb to enhance the effect.
- **Strategically placed satin sheets:** Invest in a luxurious set of satin sheets. You can seductively slip and slide as you strategically cover your flaws. For example, if you have long legs or ample breasts but carry excess belly bulge, you can drape the sheet over your tummy. This does not mean you should cling to the sheet during the entire lovemaking session. Just use this aid to help you get into the mood. It also serves as a seductive tease. Trust me—if you are at this stage of the relationship he is not going to be thinking about your belly bulge. (This also can work with the cotton sheets at your Boy Toy's place.)
- **Lingerie:** I love lingerie! There are tons of styles available to enhance your body type and personality. Think of it as the power suit of the bedroom.
- **Your best BTB pose:** Take the time to pose seductively in front of the mirror. Discover what angles make you feel hot! Notice I said you. That's because I am encouraging you to find trigger moves that you can take to the sheets. Forget fake poses that you think about while in bed. These are your sexy moves. Once you consciously become aware of what moves make you feel sensual, you can transfer that energy to your

Boy Toy. If you feel sexy, both you and your Boy Toy will benefit.

What If He's a Virgin?

You don't have to stress about making love to your younger man if he happens to be a virgin. Chances are that he is doing enough of that for the two of you. You can bet that he sees you as being sexually sophisticated. His inexperience may affect his performance big-time. In fact, many younger men get so nervous they lose their erection. They may even have a premature ejaculation, which embarrasses them to a greater degree. Rest assured, this is probably because they think you are too hot to handle. Use this awkward situation to create a tender moment for the two of you. Remain calm and comforting. You might suggest that the two of you snuggle or give each other a massage. This takes the pressure off him to perform. You also could take turns caressing each other's parts. Some Boy Toys prefer a hot BTB to make love to them on the top. They prefer you to be in control in this virgin territory. If he is not able to "come," you can still show him how to please you. The important thing is to remain kind, caring, and honest with each other. This is true intimacy. Remind him that you believe in lots of practice. Don't forget to smile.

....
Cyndi's Biggest Sexy Secret
....

Here's the deal. I've given you some great tips to seduce and be nakedly up-front with your Boy Toy. This is valuable information to incorporate into your personal life. However, let me share one of my biggest sexy Cyndi's Secrets. Forget the textbook tips! Well, I don't mean you should forget about them completely. It's just that if you spend too much time worrying about what you "should" do or how you "should" act, you become an act. Being an "act" is not very seductive. You have lived life long enough to know yourself and your body better than anyone else. That is what sets you apart from most of the younger women, who are clueless about who they are. Be honest—you probably have a basic idea of what it is about you that can win hearts. Have the confidence to tap into that core source and exploit it. Move forward with enthusiasm. That's intoxicating! Passion for life—for your life—is the biggest aphrodisiac. Discover all the components of your inner core and bring them out. For example, people tell me that I have a personality that is laden with playful mischief. I see humor in just about everything. I love to learn, laugh, and live new experiences. Yet I have more philosophical depth than my outside appearance lets on. I feel joy to be alive even when I may be in the midst of downtrodden times. I care, I love, I really live! Those are the things I communicate to a love interest. That's my own big secret.

Do I expect you to be a clone of me? No way! Coming from a family with six girls and two boys, I learned very early on to appreciate the beauty in different personalities. Each is unique, and that is hot! Perhaps you are shy and reserved. Maybe you are a flower child from the 1960s. Perhaps you are in your 30s and feel independent in the first home that you've owned. You may have children, an ex-husband, or a career that has forced you to keep the real "you" bottled up. What makes you who you are? What's *your* secret? Tap into that core. Show your younger man the part of you that is bubbling underneath like a volcano ready to erupt. Your passion for life is the sexy secret to seduction. Express it to your younger man. An older man may try to suppress your passion, whereas most younger guys want to be with you as you take the journey to your higher power.

If you have been following my Boy Toy Program from the beginning, you know that I touched on passion in Chapter 4. I hope that you have used that information to make your life more fulfilling as an individual. At this point of the program, I encourage you to take it even further. Accept the risk of slowly, and with caution, sharing your deepest passions with your younger love interest. Your relationship may blossom, or it could wilt. That is the bittersweet edge of a heart on a sleeve. However, sharing can be an incredible turn-on for him and for you. Be sure to delve into his passions as well. The art of seduction is never complete without the convergence of the mental, physical, and spiritual depth of your soul with his. Encourage it with the intimacy of passion!

Be a Dating FUNatic

It was a typical Monday morning. Chelsea, a 30-something single and ambitious stockbroker, was running late. She piled her auburn hair up high in one of those no-time-but-don't-I-look-hip clips and put on a pair of trendy black-framed glasses. Bolting out the door, Chelsea sped down the street to the neighborhood coffee shop. While yakking on her cell phone, she screeched into the parking lot. Just as she was about to swerve into one of the last parking places, she slammed on the brakes as HE cut in front of her to snatch the spot. Expletives blurted out of her lips. Steaming, she skidded into the next spot and stormed out of the car. Her colorful language was quickly curtailed the second their eyes met. He had much more brawn and was far younger than the scholarly types she usually dated. Chelsea was instantly smitten by his tall physique, long hair, and Fabio–romance novel appearance. "I'm sorry," he said. "Oh nooo problem," she calmly responded. This man was not her usual cup of tea—but then again, they were at a coffee shop. When he asked her out, she paused so as not to appear overanxious, told him yes, and smiled to herself as she thought, "hmmmmmmmmmmm—something's brewing!"

Although Chelsea never took a yoga class in her life, she didn't flinch when he suggested she attend a 7:00 P.M. class with him. Together they bended, twisted, and stretched. However, she watched him flirt with every pretzel form in the class. Friendly flirting is one thing, but exchanging phone numbers behind her back was a different matter. Her dreams of a full-bodied robust relationship died when she discovered he was nothing more than a lothario drip.

Scenarios such as these are the lament of many a single woman. If you decide to continue playing the dating game, you have some choices. Here is another one of my sexy Cyndi's Secrets. You desperately either move from one disappointment to the next with the attitude of a dating "fanatic" or take the positives out of each experience and become what I call a dating FUNatic! I personally choose the latter. Consider Chelsea, for example. It would have been easy for her to start feeling sorry for herself. She could eventually have become a bitter woman. She might even have given up on dating Boy Toys. However, a true dating FUNatic can stop and look at the situation from the outside while growing stronger from each dating experience. My friend Chelsea remembered to use my Controlled Crying technique.

As a result of releasing her hurt feelings, she focused on the positives. In spite of the bad experience, Chelsea discovered that she enjoyed yoga. She has been doing the practice now for three years. It has improved her physique, helps her to manage stress, and she is convinced it will keep her looking and feeling young forever. None of this goodness would have happened if she had maintained a negative dating attitude. A dating FUNatic is able to rise up above all the crap that comes along. Seeing the humor in all of these bad dates makes them, well—fun! Who among us doesn't want to have fun?

Bear in mind that successful dating takes two. It's also your responsibility to *be* fun. If you act like a stick-in-the-mud, your date won't have much incentive to be kind to you or even want to see you again. People are drawn to happy people. Make him want you. Make him crave you by reflecting your inner joy. This does not mean you have to hide your spitfire passions; they contribute to a fun spirit, too. One of the ways of finding joy in being single, and throughout life, is to be true to you. It also helps to be able to laugh, learn from mistakes, and embrace both the good and bad dating experiences. They can add up to a fun and pretty darn fulfilling life! Having zest for life is very sexy. It's probably another one of the best-kept secrets of being sexy and sensational!

I have to chuckle when I think of all the dates I had that went bad. There was the grieving widower who enthusiastically pounced on me on his sofa immediately after dinner at the same time his mutt repeatedly humped my leg. And the photographer who failed to tell me he was picking me up on a motorcycle to take me to a cocktail party. Although some people like making an entrance with windswept hair, this was not the ride of my life. I also think of the nice dates that have enriched me. I have basked in a room full of rose petals and candlelight and maneuvered through Monte Carlo. I've sailed into the sunset with a heroic Adonis who fed my fantasy of being cared for and protected. Oh—how I treasure the man who helped me feel so safe I could fall asleep on him as he talked about profound guy "stuff" under the stars on my patio. How fortunate I have been. Dating without a doubt has its share of fond and not-so-sweet memories. Using your fun factor can make all the difference. Now I invite you to use the following sexy Cyndi's Secrets tips to help you discover how to be a successful dating FUNatic:

- **Fun:** Fun! Fun! Fun! The word itself is fun! Make it part of your daily being. Breathe it in and breathe it out.
- **Understanding**: Be understanding. Try to look at your date from his point of view. Is he shy? Is he nervous? Is he a jerk?
- **Nicely Naughty:** When dating, it pays to be nice. Being nicely naughty with someone special can be fun, too.
- **Attitude:** Attitude is everything, baby! If you feel good about yourself, you are going to have a sexy and sensational time dating Boy Toys to your heart's content.
- **Thankful:** "T" stands for "thankful." It could also stand for "therapy." Being thankful for all your good qualities and blessings in life can help you avoid therapy, or at least make it more successful.
- **Individual:** You are special. No matter who you are dating, never be afraid to be the unique individual you are. You can't pretend forever, and eventually he will find out who the real you is anyway. This is particularly important to younger men who tend to trust your every breath.

- **Climax:** I wanted to end this chapter with a climax. The climax of the matter is this: You have choices! You can be a dating "fanatic" or a dating FUNatic. It's up to you!

Chapter 12

Dealing with Friends and Family

The Shock of It All

In many circles, it is considered shocking to date a younger man. You can pretty much count on having experiences that culminate in embarrassing moments. This chapter can help you cope with meeting his friends, your friends, his family, your family, and all the others, including the sexy Swedish shopkeeper who works in men's accessories at the local department store. You know, the one who asked for your "son's" phone number and proclaimed to your guy, "What a big glove size you have!" Don't panic! Take a deep breath and read on.

There are bound to be generational and life experience differences when you date a younger man. In fact, those variances seem to be the biggest negatives cited in my cybersurvey and interviews. However, these challenges do not have to destroy what may be a perfect match between you and your Boy Toy. Most of the couples in my survey were able to overcome the pitfalls of generational issues.

Start by dealing with the generational issues that occur within your own private relationship. That means you should try to stall before bringing his or your friends into the picture. Most important, try to avoid meeting his mother or father, and having him meet your family, until you absolutely have to. I'll address how to deal with them later in the program. Get to know him first to avoid outside influences.

Try to spend part of your private time with him working on bridging the generation gap. Expect to find differences in music, slang words, and various views of the world. You may think rap is crap while he disses disco, your secret desire. Once you look beyond these superficial elements, you can observe the relationship with eyes wide-open. Do you have similar interests? Do you share core values? Do you share the same morals? Start addressing these questions about your philosophy of life as you discover all you can about each other's generation. Only when you understand his language coupled with all the serious stuff will you be able to decide whether this relationship can work for you. You can discover whether it is purely physical, a novelty, or represents something more. The two of you can then determine what you want out of the relationship. You can decide how to shape it.

Cyndi's Secrets™

As you proceed, I remind you once again, as I have several times in this program: always be true to you! Dating a younger man can be so much of a fantasy that you forget your roots—and I'm not talking hair dye (though you may be having so much fun that you forget that appointment, too). Just as you do for your hair and makeup and clothes, find your inner true colors and stick to them.

As you discover his generation, be sure to share a part of your history and generation. This usually isn't too hard to do. Younger men often are dying to hear what you have to say. So, study each other's age-related stuff. Some of this will be fun and other parts frustrating. There are going to be differences that the two of you will never be able to mesh. There is nothing wrong with each of you having your own uniqueness. The combination of your convergence and uniqueness prepares you for the jungle out there, where you must meet each other's "others."

Friends in *His* Circle

Meeting a younger man's friends certainly can come with its share of obstacles. For example, when Florence saw her Boy Toy hanging out with his guy buds for the first time, she saw a different side of him. The mature man in a hunk's body she had come to love suddenly morphed into an immature kid. She never saw him guzzle a beer, followed with a burp. Now he acted as if it were something to be proud of in front of his boy buds. Then there are all those cute young women. Mary remembers the bronzed Brazilian beauty who sidled up to her Boy Toy at a party. This bikini-clad bombshell had the nerve to say right in front of Mary, "I like your shortie!" Mary was pissed. Little did she know that Miss Brazil was giving her a thumbs-up. Her remark was actually a compliment—young people nowadays use the term "shortie" for "the girlfriend." Nevertheless, meeting "his" friends is enough to drive a girl crazy.

Now wait! Let's do a reality check. First of all, do not forget that you are a hot BTB! Second, how much of your insecurity is manufactured, and how much is real? Men of all ages often act juvenile when they get together. This is some sort of male ritual. Don't expect that to change any time soon. This is not to say that all men behave badly when in a group. Use your judgment based on him as an individual and not his age when determining whether this behavior is acceptable to you. You can choose to avoid being around him during his boy-bud outings or suck it in and belch with the best of them. You can also opt out of the relationship if you can't handle his behavior. It is of the utmost importance that you address this early on, because these characteristics in a person usually do not change.

Regarding the constant threat of younger women, the solution is quite simple. They are not a threat! Let me clarify. The men in my survey did not care about age. It just was not an issue. In many cases, Boy Toys were not even aware that their hot BTBs were older. You might be interested to note that younger women often may be jealous of you! When that green monster starts to consume you, stop it immediately. Fight the urge to be jealous of his pretty young friends. You are never going to be 18 again. Why would you want to? Get over it!

Boy Toy Talk

"Jason was 35 when we dated, and I was 54. Originally from Boston, he came from a family that owned a prominent and established retail chain. His inherited wealth made him what I call a silver spoon. He was mature and worldly beyond his years—a dream to look at visually with a mind to match. I'm an artist and he loved to escape into my creative world. Everything was perfect when we were alone. However, I never seemed to fit in with his stuffy friends and family. At first we tried but truthfully, the people in his life became too stifling for me. Although a few blue bloods got bent out of shape with our age difference, Jason was not concerned about our age and neither was I. The breakup was more socioeconomic than an age issue. He was not about to cut those ties."

Pamela, 57

Here are a few tips to help you make it through meeting his friends.

- Start with meeting a few of his friends rather than a huge group. If a wedding or large event is approaching soon, it is even more beneficial to meet someone from his posse ahead of time so you will have someone on your side.
- Phone chats ahead of meeting his friends can help. This may take support from your Boy Toy, since younger men and women often prefer texting to talking.
- Don't try to be like the girls his age if that is not you. Showing up at a barbecue with a pierced belly button and low-rise jeans à la muffin top only makes you look ridiculous if this is not your usual attire. Of course, many young women should not wear this look, either. However, if your tummy is flatter than most at any age and this is your style, smile and go for it!
- There will be those who don't like you. Some will even stare. You can choose to ignore this if the negative response is coming from someone who is not a key figure in his life. However, if one of his meaningful friends gives you the cold shoulder, try to warm up to him or her. Ask questions and express genuine interest. Sometimes it may be that they have a natural curiosity and are looking out for their friend. You can comfort them with appreciative words and actions toward your younger man.

It can help to remember that though you are a hot BTB not everybody is going to like you, regardless of age. Unfortunately, there is also prejudice. Express your concern to your Boy Toy but be careful not to drive the point so hard that he sides with his friend. If he cares, he'll stand by you. As your love grows for each other, obstacles such as these usually become less important.

Friends in *Your* Circle

When it comes to having him meet your friends, you would think things would be easier. This is not always the case. Suddenly you find out who your real friends are. Many will be secretly jealous, while others might think this type of relationship is unnatural. Follow these tips for introducing your Boy Toy to your friends:

Cyndi's Secrets™

Many times it is the "friends" who do not accept a woman with a younger man in a relationship. This is a harsh reality of the times. To combat the loss, many couples in my survey and interviews opted to create a new set of friends. It is helpful to cultivate a new group of "our" friends.

- Share your joy with your best friend first. Let him or her know ahead of time that you have met someone special. Explain your concerns about the age difference if it is bothering you. Even if it doesn't trouble you, be sure to prepare her or him for the age difference. This is a great time to set up a quick, casual meeting. You and your younger man can meet your best friend for a quick drink, say before you catch a play. This allows a warming-up period for all involved.
- Beware of the spirit crushers. There are people who often act as if they love you and have your best interests in mind. However, this is sometimes a fraudulent front

covering up selfish motives. For example, Betsy's good friend Gina told Betsy that she was thrilled she found such an adorable younger man. Gina wished her much happiness. With a kiss and a hug she then whispered, "I have the name of a great plastic surgeon if you want to really sizzle. Don't worry—you can thank me later!" Comments such as these coming from so-called friends and loved ones are actually a slap in the face. Be aware of these "caring" people. Spirit crushers can and probably will invade your life. They may do everything possible to burst your bubble. Don't let them!

- Take your time with introducing him to a bigger group. It helps if he knows several from the group as individuals before making an entrance at a huge party or event. To show up suddenly without a warning may make your Boy Toy feel that he is in a room with piranhas. All the staring and endless questions from your friends could be uncomfortable at first.

- A Boy Toy may become jealous of your male friends. It is usually a result of his insecurity. You can try to reassure him verbally. It is even more effective to show your physical affection for him with, say, a peck on the cheek in front of his imagined competition.

Boy Toy Talk

"He is 24 and I'm in my 30s. We lived together for a year and a half. He had insecurity issues with my male friends my age, and when this occurred, he would drink and lash out at himself and me. Younger men tend to be more outgoing and passionate. The last few relationships and dates I've had have been with men younger than I . . . they were the ones that pursued me . . . I like that!"

Gina, 33

Friends in *"Our"* Circle

As time goes on the two of you can develop friendships with people that you both enjoy being with. This new circle may include some of his friends as well as some of yours. Of course, there are always new friends, too. Since both of you are mature adults, making friends should be more about common interests rather than some stupid, fabricated age barrier. For example, if you and your Boy Toy love ballroom dancing you are sure to find others with the same interest—of all ages!

The biggest factor in making friends mesh well with the two of you is the communication that exists between you. If both of you can agree to communicate up-front about your insecurities, hang-ups, likes, and dislikes, you can avoid a lot of misunderstandings.

Your friends will most likely invite the two of you to events. The communication skills that you have developed will be particularly helpful as you decide which invitations to accept as a couple. Each of you must ask yourself whether the event is something you would attend for enjoyment, or just because you have to. The two of you then can decide whether to go alone or together. You have other choices, too; you could drive separately, stay a short while, or just not go at all. Do not threaten your relationship with the problems that "others" throw at you. It is not worth it. Use communication to maintain your individuality and your relationship.

The Boy Toy Mom

Even if your Boy Toy relationship is going well, do not run down the aisle just yet. Make sure you take the time to get to know each other's families. Unless the two of you are isolated from these people, family can have a huge impact on the success of your relationship. Who is the biggest threat to BT and BTB bonds? You guessed it—in most cases, it's his mom! The Boy Toy Mom (BTM) is usually not a big fan of BTBs, especially a confident, hot BTB such as you. Do not take this personally. Be smart and avoid any chance of a surprise first meeting with her or anyone from his family. Encourage your Boy Toy to speak to her about you if your relationship is beginning to get serious. He should be sure to mention your ageless spirit—not necessarily a number! In keeping with my philosophy, I recommend that he be honest with her and tell her that there is an "age difference" without being specific. She won't be as shocked when she meets you, and in fact may be pleasantly surprised that you look younger than what she's expecting. Make the first meeting a quick one so she can get used to you. For example, he can arrange to tell her you will be with him when he has to drop off a package at her house. There's no need to draw attention to the age difference. Be cordial. You and your Boy Toy can follow up with a casual luncheon on another date after she's gotten used to the shock. With a little patience, kindness, and understanding, you may be able to push through any Boy Toy Mom obstacle. Make no mistake, those obstacles can be challenging—so let's discuss the BTM even further.

Cyndi's Secrets™

When meeting the family, especially his mom, do not dress like a sex kitten. I'm not saying that you should appear to be a different person than who you really are, but downplay your sensuality.

Meeting His Mom at Your Class Reunion

In all fairness, some Boy Toy Moms might instantly welcome you. They may even be happy to meet you at your class reunion. Sharing a trip down memory lane if you are the same age may help your cause with these women. However, even if the BTM is responding positively, it is best to remain cautious. Try not to act overly physical with your Boy Toy in front of her. For example, let's say his mom got pregnant with your Boy Toy when she was in high school. It's not a good idea to let her see you groping the leg of the boy she was carrying at the prom. Instead, choose to build on your camaraderie with this type of BTM. Truthfully, moms do not enjoy seeing their sons doing too much lovey-dovey stuff when they first meet you regardless of your age. Now the dads—later on that!

Boy Toy Talk

"When my mother heard I wanted to marry Sophie, who is sixteen years older than I am, she was dead set against it. She refused to give me her permission. At 29, I did not need permission, but I just wanted a blessing. Mom refused to come to our wedding and poisoned the feelings of the rest of the family. They all were against it and did not show up for the civil ceremony. Sophie was and still is beautiful, much younger looking than her years. My mom was against her because Sophie had two daughters from a previous marriage. She felt that it was wrong to marry a woman who was not a virgin. She led me to believe it was the scandal of marrying a divorcée with kids rather than being with a woman Sophie's age. That was twenty-nine years ago. Sophie and I are still happily married."

Clifford, 58

The Protective Mom

Many Boy Toy Moms become suspicious when they see their young son with an older woman. They put up a protective barrier. If you sense the BTM is like a mama bear trying to protect her cub, do not pounce on the young with too much furor. Give the mom a chance to get to know you. Let her see what kind of a person that you are. This takes time and patience, but it's worth the wait if you really care for your Boy Toy. Should your intentions not be pure, why are you even meeting his mom? Are you being honest with your Boy Toy? If he has introduced you to his mom, there is a good chance that he's seeing this as a serious relationship. Make sure that all involved are on the same page.

The "Fix My Son" Mom

Sometimes the Boy Toy Mom may be happy because she thinks you can help shape up her son. Say he is living at home and holds six-pack abs but doesn't hold a job. With you in his life, there may be incentive for him to get off the couch. I hope you have the sense to get out of this relationship if your guy does not mature. However, I have also heard from many women who had short and sweet successful rendezvous with younger men like this. They inspired their Boy Toys with words of wisdom and a hot body. The mom thinks her son is showing some promise of hope. You get an ego boost from this delicious hunk. Obviously, this is not the deepest connection on the planet. If you go this route, be sure it is what both of you really want. Be prepared for the consequences. You are a big girl—it's your choice.

The Jealous Mom

A common complaint I hear from people I interviewed and surveyed is that the mother can become jealous of a hot BTB. This may be an issue particularly if you are successful, good looking, and happy in love. Many times the mom realizes how awful her own life is. You may remind her of what she does not have. Perhaps her marriage is in shambles. She may have curtailed her passions with family and other responsibilities. You remind her she could have become something more, and that is depressing. Again, try to give her time to warm up to you.

The Private Chat

Sometimes the Boy Toy Mom will corner you for a little private chat. Whether her choice of words is subtle and whisperlike or an obvious attack on you, try your best to be sensitive to her concerns. This is the time for you to get off the soapbox. Back off and try to comfort her. She is, after all, a mother. You may be one yourself and know that the need for a mother to protect her children can be fierce. She may see you as the cougar predator stereotype. Her fear may be that you are using her baby for sex and plan to throw him away when you are finished. Let her know that your intentions are good. Share how much you care for her son and would never want to hurt him. Give her the chance to talk, and be sure to listen. Even though she may appear chummy, do not start giving out your life history. The goal again is to comfort her. Save the personal chatter for when you know you can trust her as a friend and the mother of your Boy Toy.

Torn Between Mom and You

The younger man often feels torn apart. He wants to please his mother and you at the same time. After all, he loves both of you. This is often the turning point in these relationships. Communicate your concerns about the BTM with your Boy Toy. You need to find out whether you really are first in his life. Both older and younger men can be a "mama's boy." However, a younger man is more likely to hang on to her strings because he hasn't lived life long enough to let go. When push comes to shove, if he is not standing up for you at this point in the relationship, you cannot expect him to change.

Her Voice Carries

Be aware that when you are not around, she is talking to him. Often this can influence his feelings about you. The BTM may plant a bad seed. If your younger man takes the bait, he may start to project her negative comments on you. Suddenly, the things he loved about you may become fodder for criticism. If you suspect a BTM power trip, ask your Boy Toy straight out if his mom talks negatively about the relationship. It's best to ask when you both are relaxed so that you don't appear threatening. If the answer is yes, the two of you need to discuss the troubling issues together. Only then can you cut through the mind play and address what his real concerns are, versus his mother's. If he denies a BTM intervention, you can apologize for the misunderstanding. It is still critical to work through his issues, which now are yours, too.

Never Speak Badly of Her

Even if he is very upset about how his mom is treating you, never speak badly of her. I repeat—do not speak badly of her! He is still her flesh and blood. It is important to communicate your honest feelings and express your hurt and disappointment to him, but never ever say anything that he can throw back at you later. Trust me—he will bring it up during every fight that the two of you are bound to have. You may hear it for the rest of your life. Work as a team rather than against each other.

The Train Wreck Mom

There is no nice way to say this. Some BTMs are a train wreck. I'm referring to the dysfunctional family where everything revolves around a controlling and manipulative matriarch. Unless you want to have a puppet master pulling your and your Boy Toy's strings, it's best to cut the rope rather than tie the knot. In the mind of a train wreck mom, no woman can ever take her place, so you do not have a chance no matter what your age. She would think nothing of destroying his happiness if it meant saving her own. She controls through guilt, often acts like a victim, and exudes a false sense of power. In truth, she is insecure and exhibits low self-worth. Do not be surprised if he adores her, since she coddles him constantly. Be prepared for the nasty comments and sneers she will give you every chance she gets. This woman is cruel and abusive. If you decide to "stand by your man" in spite of the train wreck mom's shenanigans, don't expect this behavior to end any time soon. These relationships usually do not work. Unless you are willing to put up with a lifetime of verbal abuse, the sooner you get off that track the better.

The Boy Toy Dad

Boy Toy Dads (BTDs) don't seem to harbor as much resentment toward this kind of relationship. Many men treat the situation as, "Hey, hey son—way to go"! One woman I spoke with said that after she broke up with her Boy Toy, his divorced father asked her out. He was closer to her in age and was hot for her too. Many times if the father acts unhappy about your being in his son's life it is because his wife has been giving him hell about you. Do your best to act civilized and to get along.

Adult Children

Just because you and your Boy Toy are euphoric about each other does not mean adult children, whether yours or his, are going to respond in a grown-up manner. Most of us revert to being a "kid" when we think of our mommy and daddy. It can be difficult seeing Mom with a younger man or Dad with an older woman. Expect some natural resistance. Initially the age difference may be a factor. However, the long-term success rate has more to do with the individuals involved rather than age.

Their Introduction

You and/or your Boy Toy should talk to your respective adult children individually before a meeting is set up. Express to your children that your younger man makes you happy! Expound on his good qualities as a person rather than his nice ass. If he has adult children, he should do the same about you. Share photos ahead of time so that the children are not completely shocked. Plan a small, casual dinner party, first with your children and then with his, if he has any. Stall on any combined family gatherings until everyone has a chance to get used to this new connection.

Achieving Acceptance

The biggest issue a BTB and BT usually deal with is lack of acceptance. Often happy lovers are enthusiastic about sharing their love with the adult children, initially going extremely out of their way to get involved with them. This can take a couple to the point of exhaustion. You can save yourself a lot of grief if you and your Boy Toy come to the realization that *acceptance takes a lot of time*—even years. Do not bombard the adult children with immediate overt attention. It's best to demonstrate that you are consistently genuine and caring through the long haul. For example, rather than trying to act buddy-buddy by including them in numerous activities, make your social contacts gradual. Show up at events that demonstrate the support from you and your Boy Toy, such as a marathon or auction that the adult child organized. In time, you and your Boy Toy can come to represent a combined "constant." Isn't that what most of us hope to have from our parents and loved ones?

Understanding Their Anger

To succeed at making this new extended unit work, step back and put yourself in their shoes. Following are some of the reasons why adult children are afraid of your love connection, and what you can do:

- **Afraid of being left alone:** When a Boy Toy and BTB connect, the adult children are often afraid of being abandoned. They think the new love interest is going to prevent them from being close to their parent. In fact, your children may feel you are acting like a child. As a result, you and your Boy Toy may experience resentment and total rejection. It's up to you and your Boy Toy to explain to your children individually what part they play in your life. For example, you can tell your daughter, "Mary, I'm in love with John. However, you are still my daughter and I will always love you and be there for you."

- **Who is number one:** Children of all ages often want to be the apple of their parent's eye. This is a strong issue if your children are the same age as your Boy Toy. They may even feel a new sibling-type rivalry with your Boy Toy. Who is the favorite? It creates even more stress when they think of you as romantically involved. Have the strength to tell them the truth. For example, nobody benefits if your daughter comes over to visit and is surprised to find that her old bedroom is now your Boy Toy's office. You can comfort adult children by being up-front and explaining what their new role will be. Let them know that they still play a major part in your life.

- **Jealous of love:** A daughter of the same age as your Boy Toy may even become jealous if she doesn't have a love of her own. Remind her that your Boy Toy makes you very happy. Assure her that she is worthy and deserving of her own love, which will arrive when the time is right.

- **Inheritance:** Money issues can open a whole can of worms. Let's face it, adult children worry about losing the inheritance that they feel is rightfully theirs. If you have money, your children probably are squirming; if he has the money, it's his children who are concerned. Here's the deal—each of you can do what you want with your money. However, if you and your Boy Toy are becoming permanent partners, have the respect to discuss this honestly with each other first. Let your BT know that you plan on leaving the house in Paris to your daughter. He should be frank with you, too. After you have worked out your wishes as a couple, you can comfort the kids. You could say to your daughter, "Don't worry, I would never treat you unjustly." Of course, you may choose to leave your son out of the will and simply say, "Hey bub—get a job!" I'm just saying that each situation is different.

- **Protecting you:** Sometimes the children are trying to be protective. They are acting out of their "love" for their parent. His adult children may see you as a predatory cougar, while your children may think the Boy Toy is taking advantage of you. You and your Boy Toy can express to your children that you appreciate the concern. Ask them for time to trust your judgment. Explain to them that all relationships are risky. Even if you and your Boy Toy were the same age, your children could not protect you. That is just life.

- **Lack of loyalty:** The children may think that their parent is no longer loyal to the original family model. They feel betrayed. Some children even fear that if they condone this new match, they are not being loyal to their "other" parent. Explain to the children that loyalty can evolve. By hanging on to an old family model, they are preventing the metamorphosis of an enriched life and an extended new family.

Cyndi's Secrets™

If the problems with adult children seem insurmountable, you may want to consider family counseling. In some situations, a few short sessions with an intermediary person can work wonders.

It's Your Life

Sometimes you can try to no avail—the adult children never come around. However, you and your younger man should not be afraid to let your or his children know that this is your life, and together you and he are a team. It may come down to you or your Boy Toy telling the children that they cannot run your life. Be strong about choosing to live your life the way that is right for you. Have faith that in time the adult children may come to see how happy you are with your Boy Toy and share your joy. You can only hope. Remain loving, kind, and always open.

Young Children

Fortunately, young children usually do not discriminate when it comes to age. They are looking for love and security and want you to take care of them. The usual problems that occur with an extended family are going to be there regardless of your Boy Toy's age. Interestingly enough, in my research it was 13-year-old daughters of the Boy Toy Babes who had the most difficult time accepting the younger men. These young girls going through puberty found it hard to see their mom with a younger man. Following are two scenarios that exemplify what can happen when children are against your relationship. It's interesting to note how differently these people dealt with the same dilemma, garnering different results.

"My daughter Rhiannan was 13 when I fell in love with George. I had been divorced for three years and it was hard trying to support my family as a single mom. I was 47 and he was fifteen years younger. I felt so young and alive with him. Rhiannan was so nasty to him. She would act out her anger about my relationship by behaving badly at school. I couldn't handle the constant negativity that she brought to the relationship. We were together for four years, but I eventually put Rhiannan first and broke it off. In spite of Rhiannan, they were the most loving and passionate years of my life. I often reflect on what could have been and can't help but feel regret. Rhiannan is all grown up and on her own. She is involved with a man she loves. I am alone without a partner. At the time, George pleaded with me to stay with him. I shut him out. He eventually married someone else."

Katrina, 61

"Naomi was sixteen years older than me when we met. I fell in love with her instantly. We eventually got married and still are together after twenty-some years. It was rough knowing that my mom and family were against us being together. However, what was even worse was dealing with her 13-year-old daughter. She has two daughters, but it was the oldest that gave us a difficult time. It got so tough at times; I began to wonder whether we were doing the right thing by staying together. However, the love that Naomi and I shared was so strong that we knew it would be wrong to stop. We both worked diligently to communicate to her daughter that we both love her. This was by no means an easy task. There were constant sit-down sessions. A lot of yelling and talking back. We even had to, at one point, just tell her straight out that this was our life and she could not tell us how to live it. We viewed the situation as a parental struggle. Splitting apart from each other was never an option. We made that clear to her daughter. Eventually, she came around. Now she is 40 and I am actually closer to her than with the other daughter. My wife is more beautiful than ever and I still love her and both of her daughters."

Clive, 58

Your Family

I have found that the family of a hot BTB usually does not present a problem. At this stage of your life, they know who you are. You can't fool them! They also know that they cannot change you. Usually, the BTB family is supportive and just wants you to be happy. Still, there are some issues you might need to address in terms of your family:

- **What if he hurts you?** Don't be surprised if your family worries about him hurting you. This goes back to the old stereotype of the man leaving a woman when she gets older. Forget that nonsense! You already are older, and that is not stopping him. He thinks you are hot. Be sure to reread my theory of relativity in Chapter 1.
- **Your mom:** Boy Toy Babe moms can sometimes be apprehensive about your relationship with a Boy Toy. This is perfectly understandable. After all, she came from a generation in which the ladies almost always

went for the older guy. She is used to the old stereotype that "men get better with age!" What man created that media hype, I'll never know. Give your mom some time and she most likely will come around.

- **It'sa phase:** Perhaps they think you are going through a phase. In truth—you might be. There have been men I thought I was in love with, only to discover that they were indeed a phase in my life. The important thing is that it is your phase and it could grow into something more. Whether it is short lived or long term, it is your choice to be with your Boy Toy. Explain to your family that you want to explore this relationship. If it is a phase, you intend to make it a great one!

- **What if the two of you are the house joke?** If Jay Leno can make regular jokes about Michael Douglas robbing the cradle with Catherine Zeta Jones, you can bet your family may tease you. I suggest you lighten up a little bit. As long as they are laughing in a warm and loving way, with you and not at you, go ahead and have fun. If your Boy Toy hears the jokes, it's a great way to find out whether you and he share the ever-important same humor base. If the joking never ends or it becomes mean and offensive, ask your family to curtail the "humor."

- **Rude and cruel behavior:** There are times when families may exhibit rude and cruel behavior toward your Boy Toy. Do not tolerate this. You must speak directly to the offending individual or group. Let them know that this is someone you care about, and that you expect him to be treated with the utmost respect.

Chapter 13

Is He Acting His Age?

Boy Toy Stages

When it comes to choosing a mate, you should follow your heart. However, you can follow your heart out the door if you don't consider the stages a man goes through in life. Dating a man in his early 20s sets up a different set of issues compared to a man in his 40s. I'm not trying to put the kibosh on the romantic joy that may be lifting your spirit—not at all. Nor am I contradicting my ageless love philosophy. In any relationship, you want to be sure that where he currently is mentally, and where he is going, is in sync with where you are mentally, and where you are going. A harmonious life match can take you and your Boy Toy beyond a temporary fling to the real thing.

The Early 20s

A man in his early 20s probably presents the most challenging Boy Toy stage to get through. He may be striving for independence but still have a tremendous need to "belong." This can present a problem if you do not enjoy hanging out with his friends. However, you can resolve that issue if you don't mind his absence and embrace having your own alone time. Be aware that everything he is experiencing is most likely "new." Whether it is a new school, job, or apartment, his head is swimming with stuff to think about. He may even be living at home with his parents. If this is the case, you should stall on any early parental introductions. It is best to arrange for your dates away from his house at least till you can decide how the two of you fit together. If this relationship ends up being short lived, you won't have rocked the boat unnecessarily.

Men in their early 20s often have a problem expressing themselves. I know you are going to say that most men lack the ability to say what they feel. That is true, but it is even harder in the early 20s. How can you express what you feel if you are at an age of major self-discovery? There are many life choices facing a man at this age. He often doesn't know what he thinks or feels. "What do I want to be when I grow up" is a real issue for him. His frustration with himself can often come back at you. He may love you one minute and then act totally aloof the next. Truthfully, you may be facing, in some cases, a very self-centered young man. This requires patience and understanding from you. You cannot take to heart everything he says to you. However, be careful not to let him take you for granted. Is he genuinely trying to learn about life and maturity from you, or does he consistently revert back to the "Me! Me!" mode? The answer is to trust your instincts. Ask yourself, "Does this relationship make me happy, and do I feel good?" If you feel great most of the time, it is probably on track. If you do not feel great most of the time—you know the answer!

Boy Toy Talk

"I was very young the first time I got married and was responsible for a child before I was even 20. By the time I was 36 and divorced, I was ready to go out as much as I wanted and have fun! That's when I met John. He was 22 and made me feel young. I could relive parts of my youth that I didn't experience previously. When we had been together for about a year, my mother died. She and I had been close, and I was grieving. He wanted me to do something with him and I begged off. He told me that my mother had been dead for two weeks and I should snap out of it. I knew then that he was too young and not what I needed ultimately. We lived together for another year after that until he moved away to attend business school. During the last year, I had fun and he helped pay the rent, but I did not mourn when he left and I never saw him again. For me, it gave me a chance to redo my younger days and it crystallized my understanding that I needed a commitment, not just fun. I eventually reconciled with my ex-husband after twelve years apart and we've been together since."

Linda, 57

This is not to say that all young men are selfish—of course not! In fact, many good qualities can make a man in his early 20s very appealing. He can be adventurous and a lot of fun. If you are at a point in your life where you enjoy standing on your own while he flies free, a man of this age may be the one for you. Don't clip his wings or tell him what to do, because he will quickly fly away. Of course, he should not tell you what to do, either. All of this may take some patience on your part and an honest effort on his, but if there really is love, it is possible to get through the terrible early 20s together.

Boy Toy Talk

"I'm a corporate executive of a major advertising agency. My work schedule is very demanding. I'm independent, self-sufficient, and I like my men shaken, not stirred. When I met Randy he was 23. He was delivering courier packages to my office. He was definitely shaken when he saw me. That turned me on. He is in college pre-med studying to be a physician. I admire his fortitude. He spends much of his time hitting the books, working two jobs to pay tuition, and of course hanging out with his friends. I never liked clingy men. I need my space. We have fabulous sex, fun times, intelligent conversation, and he helps me to relax. We have been together in a committed relationship for about three years and we don't see it ending any time soon."

Joyce, 40

The Mid to Late 20s

Once a man hits his mid to late 20s he usually begins to have a better idea of which direction he is taking in life. Many have started on their career path and are making a decent living. Bear in mind that this is a transitional stage. You can expect maturity levels to vary from individual to individual.

One of the most mature things a couple can do when a younger man is experiencing a life turning point is to admit that a change is taking place. If both parties are willing to try to work through the change, there is hope of growing together rather than apart. Without that effort, the relationship most likely will not work. For example, if you really cannot tolerate his excessive drinking, find out if he is willing to cut back on his own. Is he mature enough to get professional help if needed? If you decide to press through the transition, make sure you keep re-evaluating the relationship. His quarter-life crisis could last on through midlife if you don't address the problem issues head-on.

Boy Toy Talk

"When Gary and I met, he was 28 and I was in my 30s. We explored new things together (i.e., Cuban food, independent films, etc.). We both loved NBA basketball and we shared an exciting sex life. Not all was perfect though. I owned my own home, managed my finances, and was starting to further my education. I was looking to build a future. He, on the other hand, was just getting on his feet financially and was looking to enjoy his financial freedom irresponsibly. He continued a relationship with another woman while he was seeing me. She eventually had his child. I saw no place for me in that situation."

Sarah, 37

The 30s

When a man reaches his 30s, he often experiences "separation." The need to hang out with peers is not a big deal. However, he may be thinking about settling down and raising a family. This can be a real issue if you both have different ideas about children and marriage. Do not be afraid to let him know that you are happy with the number of kids you have or that you wouldn't mind another tyke. This is acceptable to do in casual conversation as you get to know each other.

Boy Toy Talk

"I think that the most difficult part has been that I am at an emotionally and spiritually stable part of my life (finally) and he is in a quarter-life crisis at the moment. It's so hard to watch at times, and so frustrating to be involved in. All I can do is sit back and let him go through it, and wonder if I should let him alone while he does. It is sucking the passion and fun out of our relationship, truthfully. When things are good, they're great. We take long walks and chat, we enjoy movies and casual days with brunch, but when they start to go south, it can be difficult. However, Eric thinks that with love we can work everything out."

Rosetta, 31

"We met in a club in Las Vegas and have been together for fifteen months. It is still going strong. For the most part, it's really just getting used to the number difference—it depends on the maturity level and life experiences of an individual. My current boyfriend is five+ years younger. The last guy I dated (who was four years older) was way more immature in every aspect. I also think my boyfriend is an 'old soul'—he can sometimes get along better with people ten or more years older than him (and my mom thinks he looks older than me . . . that helps!)"

Courtney, 32

Men in their 30s can display heightened aggressiveness, which shows up more prevalently in the business setting and spills over into their personal life. It's almost impossible to separate. He may bring his work problems home and take them out on you. You can help by remaining calm. Suggest an evening stroll that allows him to vent in a productive and healthy manner. A man in his 30s often makes things much more difficult than they have to be. You, on the other hand, have weathered enough storms that you might think, "What's the big deal?" It is extremely important that you step back and let him make his own decisions. Telling him what to do makes you seem like a "mommy" to him. It helps to have a good sense of humor as you see him struggle through experiences you can chalk up to life. Once a man is in his 30s, he usually is more secure and confident in himself. Even if he is younger than you are, his maturity level is more likely to be developed. Well, at least it should be! Have the courage to leave if he is immature and if you are not getting your needs met.

Boy Toy Talk

"I've dated older women between the ages of 35 and 47. They are more relaxed, less complicated, and less moody than women my age. . . . They are more open and enjoyable and know how to please a man."

Art, 30

Many men in their 30s seem to reach a perfect place of, as they say, getting it all together. If you find a 30-something Boy Toy who has managed to synchronize his life, snap him up. When a match takes place at this stage, you can enjoy his energy and enthusiasm. It helps to let him revel in the confidence he exudes from a career that may be thriving and emotions that are often balanced. Nurture his sense of pride and accomplishment, and he will treasure you even more. You can do this by being loving and emotionally supportive of each other rather than giving him lavish gifts. This is a time for him to make it on his own.

Boy Toy Talk

"I was 47 when I met 36-year-old Jake. He was really sexy. I own and run a Hollywood talent agency, which keeps me very busy. At first he was loving, a great lover, and protective. It lasted a year and a half. I discovered that he drank too much and became a different person. Mean! I also did not like his kids. He always wanted to make me feel beholden any time he did anything for me."

Cassandra, 49

"At 53, I had been divorced for about ten years and pretty much swore off men. They all seemed so sweet at first but eventually became manipulative. I was tired of wearing my heart on my sleeve. Then I met Sam. Sam was 32 and I couldn't imagine why he kept asking me out. He was so persistent. I liked him but he was so young. I finally agreed to go out just once, but that was supposed to be it. I thought I would get him off my back. Once I gave him a chance, I found out that he not only was good looking but he was smart, sensitive, funny, and—you know, I love him so much now that I could cry! He is so much more together than the older men that were in my life. He treats me like a goddess and with respect! We've been happily married for seven years."

Darlene, 62

The 40s and Beyond

Men over 40 are an interesting breed. Some struggle through a midlife crisis. This can create a quiet panic within. Society pressures them into believing that they should have attained a certain level of personal and business success. This insecurity can trigger the crisis. Often they dump the wife, buy the sports car, and look for a girlfriend half their age. Avoid the man going through this like the plague. Others have the immaturity of a young boy trapped in an aging body. In addition, an unfortunate percentage eventually resorts to old farthood or the kingdom of merry, dirty old men. Must a woman who's reached her 50s, 60s, or 70s on up be limited to only 20- and 30-year-olds if she wants the pleasure of a Boy Toy relationship? I think not. If you are over 50, a younger Boy Toy over 40 may be just the match for you. To be fair, there are many men over 40 who mature into marvelous Boy Toys. These men have learned from the mistakes they made in marriage, in their work, with their kids, and in life. They are now less concerned about losing "it." However, it is extremely important that a more mature Boy Toy feel that he is still at the top of his game. You can help him tremendously just by being willing to listen. The last thing an older Boy Toy wants or needs is to hear a lecture. I'm not saying be a little quiet mouse. Just be considerate.

Boy Toys beyond their 50s often prefer companionship to romance. In fact, that is what some hot BTBs desire too. Since he is younger, the benefit is that he should have the energy to do many of the fun things you want to share together. Be sure that you and your Boy Toy are up-front about what each of you expects from the relationship.

Boy Toy Talk

"We met at work. She is eight years older than I am. Our romance lasted for two years and now we are friends. The relationship was passionate and still is fun-filled. The age difference did not affect the experience at all—probably because she looks much younger than her age. We broke up because I was not interested in marriage. Compatibility is more important to me than chronological age."

Craig, 56

There are plenty of Boy Toys who are 40, 50, 60, and beyond who have an ageless attitude. These men have evolved into fine specimens. Whether you are looking for romance or companionship, the nice part about finding a younger man if you are over 50 is that you have a very wide Boy Toy range. Your Boy Toy can be 22 or 42. Choose wisely.

All Stages: The Mommy Factor

When dating a younger man, be on the look out for the "mommy factor." Immaturity is not a very attractive quality at any age. Do you constantly have to reprimand your Boy Toy or act like his mother? If your life experience is not complementing his Boy Toy stage, it probably is not a good match. These relationships rarely work. In fairness, try not to throw your age and maturity at him every time there is a disagreement.

Boy Toy Talk

"Anytime he ticked me off, I chalked it up to his inexperience! There were times I felt like his 'mommy,' simply because I had more life experience than he did. He was quite intelligent, had a photographic memory, brilliant in his work, but I had the maturity . . . and in the end that was what divided us. I may have exuded a constant air of skepticism that kept him feeling as if he needed to prove his maturity. He was 26 and I was 34."

Laura, 48

Chapter 14

Keeping the Flames Alive

Surviving Boy Toy Reality

It was late afternoon as Sacha sat sipping lemonade on her garden patio. She lazily stretched on her chaise longue and took in a cool summer breeze. It was her first chance to relax since arriving home from Paris earlier in the day. At 47, she is a buyer for a major clothing retail chain. This is her dream job, but it causes her to travel a bit more than she likes. Ken, her live-in love of one year, stood in the distance with hose in hand as he watered the gardenias—his favorite pastime. At 35, he still looks like the perfect specimen of a man she remembers from when they first met. He was shirtless and in tight jeans as she watched the droplets of sweat pour down his pumped muscular chest. At one time, she would have welcomed him taking her down right that second. On this day, she would have preferred to take him down—with a baseball bat! She can barely recall the passion that was so fierce when they moved in together shortly after they met. At the time, they believed they were destined to be together forever. He is a moderately successful artist who now takes care of her two children and manages the affairs of the household. For the most part, the arrangement works fine. However, it seems like every time Sacha comes home from her trips the house is in disarray and he hasn't completed any of the chores he promised to do. On top of that, the den has unfinished paintings strewn throughout. She holds in her frustration, as she is usually too tired to fight. Sacha feels that Ken should grow up, and she is beginning to think he is too young for her. Ken fears that Sacha is becoming frigid and that she has no clue how hectic his days can be. Fanning any flames that may remain is the furthest thing from their minds. She distances herself and makes him wait for her physical affection till she is ready. After all, he is making her wait for the cupboards to be refinished. At least the gardenias look pretty.

Holy Moses! What happened to the fire in this relationship? It is normal for relationships to hit a crossroad when reality bites, and it can bite hard. You either grow together or split. A romance that starts with a skip and a beat of the heart and fireworks everywhere may seem to fizzle. This is very common—don't panic! Of course you have lived life long enough to know this intellectually, but tell your heart the news. Here we are, grown women, and yet we act surprised every time some Romeo shows us his true colors. Many times those colors are there on the first date, but we may act colorblind.

During the early stages of a budding relationship, we try to show our best side and give each other extra attention and kindness. In time, you discover the everyday Boy Toy in all his glory, and he discovers you. The Boy Toy reality is that he is a living, breathing human being capable of making mistakes and having his idiosyncrasies. Guess what—you are not perfect either.

Consider Sacha, for example. When she met Ken, she loved his creative, go-with-the-flow style. Well, he has not changed. Now look at Ken. He believed Sacha helped him to organize and stay focused. Her take-charge attitude was a turn-on. Well, she hasn't changed either. What may have changed are the expectations and projections that they have for each other. Over time, they both let their guard down and revealed their true selves. Does this mean that their relationship is doomed? Is he just too young for Sacha? Not necessarily.

Many hot BTBs are quick to blame any dysfunction on his immaturity. Sometimes that is the case. Other times it is just a matter of doing a Boy Toy reality check. Before you delete him from your speed dial and move on to a new Boy Toy, take an honest look at whether you can both move forward to a higher-level relationship. It can happen.

I'm here to tell you that the passion a hot BTB craves does not have to end. With my Boy Toy Program, you can sustain romance and passion if you find the right Boy Toy and nurture the relationship. In this chapter, I help you discover how to keep the flames alive should you find that his reality is a complement to your own.

Breaking Barriers

As you begin to move forward, realize that you and your Boy Toy are both up against many barriers. A number of unexpected issues can fill your lives, such as new jobs, illness, death—the list goes on. If the flames are disappearing, both of you need to take a step back. Look at the relationship from each other's point of view. This is the perfect time to develop communication as well as coping skills. That means you both must really listen to each other and not just yak away. Make a conscientious effort to repeat what the other one said so that there is no confusion—kind of an honest he-said she-said. Admit that it is okay to have different opinions.

It also helps to put a problem temporarily to rest. When you address the issue again, you may both have a fresh perspective. Be aware that every relationship runs up against issues that can be stressful sticklers. You can improve your ability to cope with those sticklers if you realize that much of life is out of your control. Change what you can and accept the rest. For example, if you think he's sleeping with a woman closer to his age at work, you can confront him in a non-threatening manner: "Honey, you spend a lot of time with Sherry from the head office, and we hardly talk anymore. Is there anything between the two of you?" Expressing your concern is in your control. If he comforts you, a barrier is broken and the relationship can grow. If he refuses to give you all the reassurance you need, you can trust your instincts and get out, or stay and feel miserable. Both choices are in your control. Firing her is out of your control unless you are the boss. Patience and understanding can often help you press through to eternal passion. If the two of you choose to stay closed-minded in your private worlds, you can expect resentment, avoidance, and eventually a relationship that flickers out like a dying ember. Ken and Sacha are letting the fire go out by not talking to each other. If they hope to reignite it, they need to communicate.

Choosing a Direction

To survive Boy Toy reality you must realize that it's very normal to go from a romantic, "isn't he perfect" phase to a "what was I thinking" dilemma. Both of you must take time to connect in order to succeed. Each of you can express what is bothering you without going on the attack. Again, be very careful not to use the age card every time you disagree. Both of you must form a truce regarding what actions must be changed. You can also agree to disagree. That is healthy.

Decide to give each other a fair amount of time to make these changes. You can then each determine what direction you want the future of your relationship to take. Can you accept his reality? Can he accept yours? Okay, here is my favorite word again: choice. It's all about choice.

Cooking Where It Counts

My friends and family often tease me for not being much of a cook. However, it's never been a problem in any of my relationships. I love to joke, isn't that why God gave us restaurants? To keep the flames alive in a Boy Toy relationship, your prize-winning French soufflé may not necessarily be the best recipe. Boy Toys usually do not believe the old saying that the stomach is the way to his heart. In fact, many of these Boy Toys are excellent cooks in their own right. Their moms, who often work, taught them well. Trust me: it is far more important to "cook" where it counts! Following are some key ingredients to help spice up a long-lasting stew.

Great Sex

When you first become involved with a young hunk, it is very easy to devour each other as if in a half-starved fast-food frenzy. Eventually the discerning palate craves more. Try these tips to turn your sex life into a loving long-term fine-dining experience:

- **Embrace your body image.** Earlier, I talked about the importance of building a healthy body image. As a relationship gets past the initial stages of attraction, maintaining your confidence can become even more challenging. As time goes on, it may be even more important to unleash the goddess within. Never, ever, let her disappear.

- **Relax, it's okay!** Many times after the initial lust of a Boy Toy wears off, a woman may start to feel guilty about her Boy Toy pleasure. The stereotype of a woman acting as a cougar predator, hunting younger men strictly for sexual power and control, may mess with your mind. This is totally different from the playful prowl of a hot BTB. It is not wrong to have a loving sexual relationship with a younger man. Release your inhibitions and free yourself to enjoy!

- **Nurture your desire.** You can nourish your sexual pleasure as a loving couple by creating situations that bolster your arousal and his. This could be as simple as going to the restaurant where you had your first date. Let him take you to a baseball card show even if it's not your cup of tea. He might be so excited to share his love of a 1955 rookie card that you score big-time between the sheets.

- **Try to forget.** If you take disagreements to bed with you, the passion cannot flourish.

- **Communicate each other's desires.** Boy Toys are extremely willing to please sexually. This is true in both long- and short-term relationships. Light his fire by asking him what he likes, too.

Cyndi's Secrets™

Humor can be sexy. Do not be afraid to have a giggle in the midst of lovemaking. This is particularly important in a long-term relationship. It keeps the love connection fresh and fun. That is, as long as you aren't smirking if he has shrinkage. Men never like that!

- **Be considerate.** The pressures of everyday life can take its toll on each of you. Taking time to let each other chill can prevent frozen behavior in bed. It could be as simple as a daily talk in your Jacuzzi or as complex as a planned trip to Hawaii.
- **Protect yourself.** Nowadays making love to a Boy Toy or any man can be a life-and-death choice. Moving forward into a long-term relationship may make you lax about latex. Before the condom comes off, be absolutely sure that both of you are free from sexually transmitted diseases, or at least aware of any that you might have. Be willing to make the commitment of sexual monogamy for the long haul. Have a healthy conversation up-front so that there is no misunderstanding.

Feed Your Fantasies and His

The imagination is a wonderful thing. It can help you cook where it counts. Let it take you to the place in your mind that is special only to you and your Boy Toy. Feel free to explore each other's fantasies. Try these tips to trigger your sexual creativity:

- **Just do it!** When a couple is falling in love, they often drop everything at the opportunity to make love. As time goes on, some put other things first. "Hold on, hon, let me finish this chore" or "Our guests will be over shortly" are but two of the excuses given to put off lovemaking. Being spontaneous can go a long way in preventing your sex life from ending up in a rut.
- **Create anticipation.** It is very seductive not knowing what is coming next. Each of you can take turns

being in charge sexually. This can add newness to your lovemaking. Many couples enjoy the erotic sensation of the unknown. Of course, this is perfect for a long-term relationship where trust is established. Sexual anticipation can whet the appetite for thrilling lovemaking. Each of you can have it your way.

- **Explore new frontiers.** Many times the younger man is not as experienced as you are in bed. Other times he may be the one who has been sexually around the block. This can happen if you were in a long marriage with a sexual dud. None of that matters now that you and your Boy Toy are together. Do not be ashamed to share fantasies and to play them out.

- **Let him enjoy foreplay.** It's no secret that women need foreplay. However, one of Cyndi's Secrets to sexual bliss is to treat him to foreplay too. That means not only physically but mentally as well. For example, say you are rushing to get ready for his company Christmas party while he sits in front of the set. You could scream out at the top of your lungs, "Harry—empty the dishwasher—now!" Instead, run out in the living room a little frazzled while wearing your tiny lace tap panties and no top. Quickly blurt out, "Honey—can you please empty the dishwasher? I'm in a hurry!" Then quickly scamper out of the room. The unexpected distraction gives him reason to mentally relish foreplay with you the entire night. Oh, and the bonus is that he probably will put the dishes away!

- **Discover what time of the day he enjoys sex best.** If you can tap into his schedule whenever possible, it can help to keep the flames alive.

Cyndi's Secrets™

Recent research shows that sex is a good workout. It gets the heart racing and muscles flexing. You can burn as many as 15,000 calories per year by having intense sex three times a week. That can equate to approximately four pounds per year.

- **Both of you should be good to go all the time.** Obviously, this is not always practical. However, taking care of each other's needs ups the excitement in a relationship.
- **Phone sex can help.** With so many people traveling for work and long-distance relationships being a reality, phone sex can help to ignite sparks when couples are apart. Do not be afraid to express your sexual intimacies on the phone. Dirty talk via the phone line is enticing. Just don't press the speaker button while at your office.
- **Naughty is nice.** In my survey, I heard from many Boy Toys who succeeded in long-term relationships. They raved about how much they love the sexual naughtiness of their hot BTB! In our culture, it is easy to forget that being a little naughty with your love can stimulate the relationship. Once you fall in love, being a bad girl in bed can be good.
- **Accept pleasure.** Do not be afraid to enjoy the lovemaking experience. You deserve to release your inhibitions and partake of all your desires. Let him please you.

Location, Location, Location!

In real estate, we hear about the benefits of a good location. Here are just a few places to consider lovemaking. Perhaps you have your own favorite hot spots. Have fun!

- Your good old-fashioned bed is a standard pleasure chest.
- A semi-public place can up the excitement.
- Try the shower, the pool, and even your sprinkler after dark.
- Enjoy making love to each other in front of a mirror. Let's face it, he is a Boy Toy and you are a hot BTB! It's a great sight!
- The classic pool table offers some interesting possibilities.
- Try the kitchen counter—now that's cooking!
- Be adventurous with a fun piece of furniture
- Etc., etc., etc.—use your imagination!

Cyndi's Secrets™

Hot BTB apparel can determine how far a couple can take their safe and playful sexcapades in semi-public. A short flirty skirt promotes easy access in a parking lot compared to when she wears her snow leggings, parka, and boots.

There are also places where you may want to avoid making love. Sometimes, we want to replicate a scene from a romantic movie but it doesn't play out quite as well in real life. Here's why a few spots are less than sexy:

- The grass can be prickly and full of bugs.
- The skies aren't that friendly. It's true that the mile-high club was thriving in the 1990s, but since 9/11 you can forget the hookup in the clouds.
- A wood floor can give you splinters or friction burn.
- Avoid doing it in front of your Web cam unless you don't mind the entire world seeing your lovemaking!

Rekindling the Romance

To keep the flames alive, do not depend solely on sexual romps. These moments of heated passion may only fizzle if the romance is gone. Don't worry; you can rekindle that warm feeling. My parents taught me this lesson—never stop dating! It is too easy to get overly comfortable with each other or put so much emphasis on work or the children that you forget your mate's needs. That can spell disaster. Boy Toys have grown up in a generation that is far more casual than yesteryear. Many have no problem coming home and existing in front of the PlayStation. BTBs can get too comfy too. Excessive reality TV shows coupled with ice-cream cartons may be your demise. My mom and dad scheduled "dates" regularly—at least twice a month. It didn't matter whether times were tough or not, she got dolled up and he was totally into her. Remember to make it an adult affair—no kids! Try these dating tips to rekindle the romance:

- **Dining dates:** Scheduled or spontaneous dining dates can rekindle those warm feelings of why you fell in love. It is essential to understand the difference between just eating and a dining date. You "eat" for survival, but you should "dine" to keep each other's heart content. Many couples like revisiting a favorite restaurant or exploring a new establishment. Dining dates can work also with a home-cooked meal or carryout shared by candlelight. The conversation is best when it's slow and focused. Get totally into your BT, and him into you.

- **Breakfast in bed:** Treat each other to a lazy morning of breakfast in bed. Spend time relaxing, reading the paper, sharing stories, and being into each other. Let children know that if you shut the door, they should not enter.

- **Getaways:** Whether it's a day, a weekend, or two weeks, getaways are a wonderful way to rekindle romance. Unfortunately, many couples return home to the same old routine. To benefit from your trip, make a conscientious decision to talk to each other about why the escape helped or why it did not. Try to develop ways to establish a positive carryover into your daily life. For example, Spencer fell in love all over again with Penny while they were in the Bahamas. She was free to listen to his dreams, since there was no work to distract her. After the trip, he told Penny how much it meant that she listened. Penny now makes time to hear what her BT has to say. Remember not to pack in too many activities during a getaway lest you miss the point of getting into each other.

- **Simple moments:** Take in the moonlight or a walk in the park. Catch a play or visit a museum. Share a movie or simply watch the same TV show on the same TV set. It may be one of the oldest clichés, but it is true: take time to stop and smell the roses.

- **Visit each other's work environment:** Work usually takes up a huge amount of time and is often a big part of our makeup. This is why showing up is a great way to exhibit interest. Meeting for lunch or just stopping by to see the new computer system can up the romance. Now you have a fresh set of topics to discuss. You also show each other's work family that the two of you are indeed committed to each other.

Reconnecting and Re-establishing the Bond

Earlier in the Boy Toy Program, we discussed how important it is to live a balanced lifestyle. I introduced you to my M.B.S. System (Mind, Body, Spirit) to show you how you can unleash the goddess within. It's exciting to use this information to help you develop as an individual. However, for you and your younger man to have a successful partnership, you must also connect to each other on these three levels. Let me explain. Most likely, when you met your Boy Toy, the two of you formed a good fit because you were balanced as a couple. His M.B.S. System balance was in sync with yours. Over time, it is normal to experience a shakeup in this equilibrium. Couples can grow apart if the turbulence is not addressed. You can keep the flames alive if the two of you continue growing mentally, physically, and spiritually, in unity. Follow these tips:

- **Mind reconnection:** Mentally stimulate each other. Discuss the stuff you love, such as history, trivia, politics, religion, or your evolving life philosophy. Challenge current thought patterns with topics of the day. Embrace the opportunity to learn from each other.
- **Body reconnection:** Both of you need to take care of your bodies physically, inside and out. Continue to let each other know how attracted you are. If you need

reassurance and he is slipping in that department, do not be afraid to let him know.

- **Spiritual reconnection:** To connect spiritually is a very deep bond. This can occur by praying together, sharing a silent meditative moment in the same room, or expressing feelings. It may even be the simple squeeze of a hand. You know—when his mom insults your potato salad and you both hold your breath. Maybe no one else sees this hand squeeze, but you and your Boy Toy are connected. Sharing beyond the physical realm is spiritual.

Nurturing this relationship may take effort on the part of you and your boy toy. Together you can use the M.B.S. System to reconnect and re-establish your bond. Take Summer for example. She was 35 when she met Danny. He was nine years younger. They were married for thirteen glorious years before he passed away in a terrible car crash. She recently shared with me how she and her beloved Boy Toy kept their flames alive. In her words:

"It was the heat between the two of us that was the key to our success. A heat that goes beyond a body that sags or a room filled with others—it's the entire connection."

Chapter 15

Making Ageless Love Last

The Permanent Partnership

I always love hearing the stories about couples who really make their relationships work for the long haul. I don't mean the ones who coexist, but the ones who maintain a deep eternal light shining for each other. My mom and dad were such a couple. I remember one night not too long before dad died. He was in the hospital and a nurse called my mother's house close to midnight. I was staying with her. We both jumped for fear that something had happened to him at such a late hour. After handing the phone to my mom, I expressed a sigh of relief when I saw a slow, soft smile sweep across her weary face. She transformed into a happy young girl, giggly in love, right in front of my eyes. I never saw anything like it! Soon I found out that my dad expressed his love for my mother in complete detail to his nurse. He even retold the entire story about how they met. It was at a wedding. During the reception, my mother, without another thought in her mind, headed straight up to my dad while he stood at the bar with his buddies. She coyly said, with a touch of being flirty, "I knooow yooou!" If you knew how shy my mother is, you would realize what a brave and remarkable move that was. Her delightful manner let him catch her. They danced all night. He refused to let any other man cut in. Dad went on to tell the nurse how mom feared accepting his marriage proposal because he was eleven months younger. Of course, I had heard the story told a million times in my life, but not like this. The nurse found it so captivating and romantic that she felt compelled to call my mom immediately. Now that Dad has died, Mom often recalls the phone call from that night. I see her face display that same smile as she relives his deep expression of love for her. I often think how tragic it would have been if she had not taken the leap of faith and committed to making a marriage work with a younger man. Remember, that was in the 1940s, when even a year was considered older. Do not let the age of someone you love prevent you from making love last.

In this chapter, you'll discover tried-and-true secrets that can lead to a successful partnership between you and your special Boy Toy. Believe in your heart once and for all that it is never too late.

The Honesty, Loyalty, and Trust Bond

If you plan on investing in the future of your relationship, an honest, loyal, and trustworthy bond can pay the biggest dividends.

Honesty

As a hot BTB you have probably been raised to hold up honesty as a high virtue. What mature woman doesn't remember the iconic role model "Honest Abe"? Sadly, today Boy Toys mostly think good old Abe represents a reason to shop at Best Buy in February. They have grown up in a society that accepts dishonesty as part of the norm. Consequently, if you believe he is worthy of your love, you may have to teach him about honesty. Explain to him the importance of sharing experiences, secrets, and just about everything with each other. He needs to know that if there is no honesty, there is no relationship. I always say I want the truth, even if it hurts. Let him know not to partake of any lies, even by omission. These are still just that—lies! For example, if your Boy Toy tells you that he did not have sex with another woman when in fact he participated in oral sexual pleasure but no intercourse, then it is a lie. The two of you must work toward a safety net where you both are free to say whatever you feel without attacking each other. He will welcome your honesty as well.

Telling the truth does not grant you a pat on the head just because you confessed. It does not make the wrongdoing go away. Many people feel that confessing should spare them from any emotional discord. Come on! You should tell the truth because it is the right thing to do.

Trust

Many Boy Toys tell me that older women get jealous too easily. These younger men don't understand why you feel this way, because they think you are hot. In most cases, you should not worry. You can't expect to know where your partner is or what he is doing every second of the day. That is where the trust comes in. With trust, there is no need to keep checking up. Perhaps it is time to relax about the age difference and have faith in your Boy Toy. However, if trust is broken, it can be very hard to repair. The relationship guidelines change slightly. For example, if he is caught cheating, he needs to win back your trust. He needs to "allow" you to check up on him, which can serve as a temporary comfort. It helps if he goes out of his way to show you that he is yours exclusively. Ask him to call you more frequently or do whatever it takes until there is trust again—if possible. Many older women in this situation begin to feel jealous. That's because catching him in a lie naturally makes your antennae go up. This can increase your need for constant reassurance, which he can come to resent. Allowing him to call that need "jealousy" takes away from his responsibility to comfort you about the lie. Do not attribute your awful "jealous" feelings to being older. This is not entirely jealousy. It's primarily a lack of *trust*. Get it back or get out!

Cyndi's Secrets™

We always hear that we should forgive and forget. Forgiving is good. However, there are times when you should not forget. For example, if your younger man is abusing you, forgive to help you heal, but please do not forget. Get help!

Loyalty

Loyalty means you can count on each other. Your word is important, and you know you can depend on your partner. Many older men think that as long as they are "loyal" to their wives, it is okay to cheat. They often equate being loyal with being the financial provider. Younger men seem to understand the difference between loyalty and trust. Perhaps it's because most Boy Toys make less money than their BTBs. Click on Webster.com and review those two terms with your partner before making a commitment.

Communication

Let's explore how good communication skills can help make a partnership with a younger man last. Try these tips:

- **You each need to listen.** Sometimes during a fight a Boy Toy lashes out and yells. He may feel it is his primal right as a man. Not to be outdone, you may view him as being immature because of his age, and you scream even louder. He yells, you scream, and we all shout sometime, "You're not listening!" Either the person is genuinely not listening or he or she cannot accept the fact that there is a different opinion. Learning to listen can save a lot of relationships. The solution is to agree that it is sometimes okay to disagree. The beacon of light is that the women in my study almost unanimously raved about the listening skills of their Boy Toys. Again—BTMs taught their sons well.

- **Don't interrupt.** Ladies, I hate to say it, but dealing with our chatter without a breath in between sentences is one thing that some guys find difficult to handle. It's very important to stop talking and let your Boy Toy speak. Because he is younger than you are, he really cares what you think. Therefore, he wants to get everything out so he can then hear what you have to say. As far as him interrupting you—Boy Toys generally do not interrupt as much as older men, which is cool. In a successful partnership, both voices need to be heard!

- **Don't just hear what you want to hear.** Sometimes Boy Toys do not have the patience to deal with an entire argument. They are young and quick to move on to the next topic. Consequently, they may hear only what they want to hear. That's because for them, daily communication often requires only a short attention span, thanks to instant messaging (IMs), texting, and sound bites. Of course, hot BTBs can be high-tech too, but a good number of us did not grow up with it. The transition between in-depth conversation and a Nextel moment is easier for us. The salvation is that since Boy Toys are good listeners, you can ask him if he indeed heard what you had to say, and he won't be offended. Oh—don't forget to hear the "message" behind his words, too!

- **Don'tplan your next sentence while your partner is talking.** BTBs are often guilty of this. You may get impatient with your younger man and tune out while he is constructing his next thought. Boy Toys usually do not have as much life experience as you. This means your cognitive ability could be more developed. This does not mean that you are necessarily smarter, but that you have evolved through a stage he still has to go through. Give him the chance to gather and express his thoughts with 100 percent attention. It is rude to be rehearsing your lines while he is talking. Of course, you should expect him to be attentive to you as well.

- **Paraphrase back what your partner just said to you.** It lets your partner know that you are listening. This is classic communication. It crosses gender and generations. Repeat, repeat, and repeat until you both know what the other one is thinking.

- **Do not respond with your belief until you are sure what your partner meant.** Because he is younger, you may assume that your belief is wiser. He, on the other hand, might think that your thoughts are old-fashioned. The two of you have to make a grown-up decision to cut out the age excuse crap. Only then can each of you really understand what the other is thinking, make a respectful response, and then come up with a resolution—together!

Touching

Now that we have touched on communication, let's communicate about touching. Intimacy through touch distinguishes a loving long-term partnership from just friendship. It could be the gentle arm on a shoulder, a kiss at the mall, or hot, steamy sex on a rainy Saturday afternoon. The nice thing about a relationship with a Boy Toy is that sexually the two of you probably are better matched as a couple than if he were with a woman his age, or you with an older man. Of course, touch goes beyond the sexual. It is the union of your mind, body, and spirit, consummated as one, that can make a relationship stay on fire forever. Pleasing each other is of the utmost importance. If the two of you are matched physically, it sure does make it easier!

Humor

Laughter is the best medicine. Sometimes there are generational gaps that affect what each of you thinks is funny. You may laugh hysterically at classic *Laugh-In* episodes. Your Boy Toy probably doesn't know all of the history attached to the humor that made the show work. There are also gender differences. I personally never got fart humor, but most guys love it. This does not mean that all is lost when dating the younger man. Humor is not only about telling jokes. It is looking toward the lighter side of life and celebrating joy together. Having a similar humor base—sharing fresh, positive, and funny takes on life—can take you from fighting to kissing and hugging playfully!

Respect

In a relationship, both partners show respect by being supportive of each other. This is a big deal to Boy Toys. In fact, I just interviewed an energetic 30-something Boy Toy last night. He couldn't stop expounding about how he loves the way his hot BTB believes in him! She makes him feel that he can achieve anything. The younger women he has dated in the past left him depressed about never seeming good enough. Hot BTBs also need respect. There's nothing like a big dose of adoration from a younger man who totally looks up to you for your accomplishments and, more important, for being you! Respect means you work as a team, yet accept and support each other. For example, if your younger man makes less money than you do and he does not get the job promotion he expected, let him know you are proud that he tried his best. Here are some tips to help ensure respect.

No Game Playing

I hate game playing. It is childish. Don't do it! It is very easy for a hot BTB to use age as a trump card over everything. You are, after all, the more experienced. This puts you in a position to be manipulative and abusive. For example, let's say you don't want your Boy Toy to go back to college because you fear he'll meet someone his own age. Rather than telling the truth, you might go into a whole song-and-dance routine about how he would be wasting his time. Even worse, you might tell him that he is not smart enough. It may feel good to get your way, but it is totally disrespectful.

Of course, he should not play games either—except maybe Twister alone with you!

Who's on First?

To show respect for each other, you need to put your partner first. This way the relationship can reach an incredible equilibrium. Many times one partner gives more than the other does. That can be typical of a relationship with some older men. However, Boy Toys often love to please you. For the most part, they have an easy time putting you first. They look up to you and appreciate your success and individuality. Be sure to assure your younger man that he is first in your life, too.

Boy Toy Talk

"He may have been nine years younger, but he respected who I was and my successes in life. He was actually proud of my notoriety in my profession. Because I was already there when we got together, there was not ever any competition between us. When I think of the level of self-assuredness that he must have had to approach me, I knew that he was extraordinary. Most men were intimidated or competitive. I loved the level of respect he gave me. I did not have to fight for it."

Marilyn, 60

Fighting Fair

When a relationship goes in the direction of long term, you can pretty much expect to discover the things that make both you and your Boy Toy vulnerable. Out of respect, you must never use that precious information in a fight. Say a younger man is climbing the ladder of success but hasn't quite gotten there. It would be cruel to call him a complete loser during an unrelated fight. It is also unfair if he shouts out of spite, "nobody wants an old hag like you." Decide not to attack each other. Stick with the issues. Fight fair!

The Last Word

Having the last word is not always the most important part of a loving partnership. This is something hot BTBs have to remember. Let's face it. We are strong and confident and usually like to have our way. Although these are good qualities, you should balance that strength with a protective shield for your younger man's feelings. Of course, your Boy Toy should respect you, too. So many things in life are trivial in the grand scheme. Giving in or surrendering on occasion can do wonders for your bond. Just let go and move on from the stupid stuff.

It's Never Too Late

If you think you are too old to find love or to enjoy a relationship with a younger man, perhaps you should think again. I recently had the opportunity to interview Gretchen and Walter. This is their story:

Gretchen barely thought about being in her 70s. She was too busy charting her future. However, when her loving husband of forty-two years passed away suddenly, she had to find a way to make her way back into life. They both loved their home in northern Michigan, but now, with him gone, Gretchen felt alone and isolated. Her two sons were grown and the rest of the family was far away. She decided to sell the couple's house and move into an apartment. With her husband gone, Gretchen had to pick up the pieces. After allowing herself to have a grieving period, she decided that at the age of 72 it was time for her to have it her way. She got a job at Burger King.

As a hostess, this was the perfect opportunity to be with people and keep her mind off of her own problems. She delighted in talking with her customers. One in particular stood out. His name was Walter. Walter was a dapper gentleman with a quirky manner mixed with a suave charm that the ladies loved and men admired. Every time he came in, she enjoyed his friendly manner. However, she could not help but sense a deep sadness buried underneath his exterior. Gretchen later found out that Walter's wife and two of his daughters died within a short time of each other. No matter how hard he tried to hide it, the loneliness in his heart was weighing on him.

Over time, their friendship blossomed and even though Walter was only 56, Gretchen found him much more interesting and fun than most of the men her age. Without giving it a second thought, she asked him to join her in a weekly dance class. This was not an official date, and they both drove separate cars. However, at the end of the first class he planted a big kiss on her lips as they said good-night at her car. He then declared, "I love you, Gretchen!" She replied, "You mean like love thy neighbor?" Walter was impressed with Gretchen's wit and quick mind. They began officially dating. She once asked him why he never invited her out for coffee. He said, "Why go for coffee when we are at the Burger King?" The truth is he was afraid that she would not want to go out with him. Walter and Gretchen fell in love. Their courtship lasted three years and they were married one Valentine's Day in the presence of family and friends. They have now been happily married for thirteen years. She is currently 88 and he just turned 72.

Gretchen and Walter are amazing. I interviewed them each separately and then together. They are truly an inspiration for all of us. Gretchen is without a doubt a hot BTB! She is tall and statuesque with the beauty and grace of a gazelle. Her presence radiates the essence of a former Vegas showgirl, still very sexy and confident about living a full and rich life. Walter totally adores her. He's never known so much love, attention, and generosity from anybody. Together these two young-at-heart lovebirds are living examples of what my Boy Toy Program can mean for the long haul. In a nutshell—it's never too late to find love!

What is the secret? Gretchen and Walter both believe that their faith keeps them strong. They handle disagreements by talking them out as calmly as possible rather than running from the problem, and they resolve issues with decisions that are best for "the two of us." You and your Boy Toy should do the same. Try to stand up to any problem. There is no room for selfish thinking in a loving relationship.

It helps to have common interests and activities that you enjoy doing together. This is even more important as you go into your later years, when you each will have more time. For example, Gretchen and Walter play in a kitchen band at various nursing homes. Often there are people in the audience who are younger than these two but appear to be much older. What a great reminder about the importance of taking care of one's health and maintaining a positive attitude!

Gretchen believes, as do many of the women I spoke with and surveyed, that being with a younger man has helped to keep her feeling and looking younger. What happens is that the younger man has no concept of you being older. He assumes you can keep doing everything just as you always have. For example, Gretchen, who lives in the woods with Walter, still splits wood and handles a wheelbarrow. She always has. They've done this for years. Being active can do more for an ageless spirit than any amount of plastic surgery ever could.

Boy Toy Talk

"Walter and I still try to keep our romance alive. We have a trailer on our wooded property and periodically we spend a few nights out there. It's like a little escape for the two of us."

Gretchen, 88

Your age does not predicate whether you can have a Boy Toy or not. It also does not determine how long your love can last. At the age of 88, many a woman stops and reflects on her life as if it were over—not Gretchen! She is living proof that ageless love can exist and even more important, it can last. It's all about making a commitment to each other. You must be willing to communicate and compromise. Don't forget to laugh. You deserve to have a loving relationship, and you *can* have it. Gretchen and Walter represent new hope for modern times. If you choose to find a Boy Toy, a meaningless number no longer limits you. For once and for all, breathe a sigh of relief—love is ageless!

Epilogue

My written word is winding down, but this is only the beginning. Now it is your turn. Yes—Cyndi's Secrets Boy Toy Program really lives on through you. You've got the tools in your hands to find the man of your dreams based on your choice. Friends tell me that I have a black belt in dating. Rich, poor, old, or young has never been an issue with me. I've always looked for the total quality within the person. With my Boy Toy Program, I know that I will never be desperate, and neither should you. I sincerely extend my good wishes. Whether you are married or single, you are special. Love is ageless! Shout it out!

Go forward with the knowledge that you are a hot Boy Toy Babe. You now have more options than ever before. Enjoy your life experiences! Some will be good and others painful, while many will be fun. Live, my friend—really live!

Please keep in touch with me, because I do care. I am continuing to gather information about Boy Toy relationships. This can help other women. Check out my Boy Toy Program site at *www.datingtheyoungerman.com*. You can also sign up for my free Cyndi's Secrets E-tips at *www.starglow.com*. Check out other products and services from my company, STARGLOW Productions, Inc. Feel free to e-mail me at *Cyndi@starglowonline.com*. So, this is not goodbye but hello. Let me hear from you. Hot BTBs rule!

Index

About the Author

Cyndi Targosz is a celebrity image consultant, relationship adviser, nationally recognized lifestyle counselor, and motivational speaker certified by ACE, AFFA, and AALC. She is the bestselling author of several books including *Ten Minute Tone-ups for Dummies*, *Erase Your Waist*, *Your Best Bust*, and *The Only Diet Book You'll Ever Need*. Her fitness video and audio programs have sold over half a million copies. She just launched the new Cyndi's Secrets fitness DVD series.

A graduate of Wayne State University, Cyndi obtained her degree in speech pathology and anatomy and physiology. Her professional background includes work as a comedic actress, model, dancer, radio personality, voiceover artist, and singer. These many experiences have shaped Cyndi's core belief of enjoying the journey with passion while setting realistic goals. She has successfully incorporated this philosophy into her M.B.S. System (Mind, Body, Spirit), believing that the mind must be centered, the body must be cared for, and the spirit must be fed. Cyndi is president and CEO of her own company, STARGLOW Productions, Inc. Her celebrity clients include Hollywood actors, actresses, models, and athletes, among others. Her list of corporate wellness clientele has included major firms such as Pacific Bell, Kaiser Permanente, Royal Caribbean Cruises, Volkswagen of America, and many more. The contribution of Cyndi's time and talents has been appreciated by numerous charitable organizations, among them the American Cancer Society, the YWCA, and the Girl Scouts of America. Cyndi was also selected by famous modern-day pin-up artist Kent Steine to pose for the creation of "The American Spirit" pin-up poster. She raises funds for our veterans and armed services groups through its sales. Cyndi is a frequent guest expert on numerous radio and television programs. Her appearances have included *Good Morning America*, Fox TV, QVC, NBC News, and *Donahue*. Visit *www.starglow.com* for more information about Cyndi Targosz, and *www.datingtheyoungerman.com* for more dating tips.